MAN OF LA MANCHA

MAN
OF
LA MANCHA
A Musical Play

by

Dale Wasserman

Lyrics by

Joe Darion

Music by

Mitch Leigh

Random House   *New York*

6 8 9 7

Photographs by Entertainment Photography, Inc.
Courtesy of Arthur Cantor

Library of Congress Catalog Card Number: 66-21454

MANUFACTURED IN THE UNITED STATES OF AMERICA

A NOTE ON
MIGUEL DE CERVANTES

Like his contemporary, William Shakespeare, Miguel de Cervantes y Saavedra lived a life only sparsely documented, many years of which are veiled in shadow. These things are known: he was born in 1547 to a proud but impoverished hidalgo family; he was a soldier, suffered serious wounds at the battle of Lepanto, was taken captive and spent five years as a slave in Africa. Above all he loved the theatre; in twenty years he wrote some forty plays, none of which were successful. In 1597 he was excommunicated for "offenses against His Majesty's Most Catholic Church," narrowly escaping more drastic punishment. He served at least three, and possibly five terms in prison on various charges. Aging, infirm, an utter failure, he undertook the writing of *Don Quixote* to make money. Volume I, published in 1605 when Cervantes was 58, brought him fame but little profit. Volume II, appearing ten years later, insured his immortality as author of the world's greatest novel, but he was already broken in body if not in spirit. He died in 1616, within ten days of the death of Shakespeare. His burial place is unknown.

Preface

MAN OF LA MANCHA was born fortuitously and underwent several metamorphoses before it was exposed to a New York audience. It had its inception in Madrid in 1959 when I read in a newspaper that my purpose in Spain was research for a dramatization of *Don Quixote*. The item was laughing-matter, for like the great majority of people who know *Don Quixote*, I had never read it. Madrid seemed a place appropriate to repair of that omission, however, so I waded in, emerging from Volume Two with the conviction that this monument to human wit and folly could not, and should not, be dramatized.

What *had* snared my interest was not the book but its author. For one learns that the life of Miguel de Cervantes was a catalogue of catastrophe. What sort of man was this—soldier, playwright, actor, tax-collector and frequently jailbird—who could suffer unceasing failure and yet in his declining years produce the staggering testament which is *Don Quixote?* To catch him at the nadir of his career, to persuade him toward self-revelation which might imply something of significance concerning the human spirit—*there,* perhaps, was a play worth writing.

I wrote it first for television in a ninety-minute version. It was produced with considerable éclat and garnered a number of awards but left me profoundly dissatisfied, for the strictures of television and its assertive naturalism had defeated both my design and intentions. I thereupon re-wrote it for the Broadway stage and it was promptly op-tioned. But I felt a sense of relief when the option period ran out without production, for I knew that while it might conceivably have been successful I still should have deemed it a failure. The play had not yet achieved the form which the material demanded; a form disciplined yet free, simple-seeming yet intricate, and above all bold enough to ac-complish that ephemeral objective which is called "total theater." My brooding on the matter had brought me to the edge of an inescapable conclusion when Albert Marre (whom I had never met) telephoned to say, "Your play is superb, but it *must* become some sort of a musical."

Precisely.

The adventure began. I use the word advisedly, for the writing of *Man of La Mancha* was an adventure, in form, technique, and in philosophy. My collaborators, Joe Darion, Mitch Leigh, and Albert Marre made enormous contributions as we groped our way toward a kind of thea-ter that was, at least within the boundaries of our experi-ence, without precedent.

It would be heartening to say that the finished play im-mediately ensnared the interest of producers and backers. It didn't. They regarded it as too radical, too "special" and, most crushing of all, too intellectual. *Man of La Mancha* floundered rather than marched toward production, sus-tained only by the tenacity of those among us who shared the Quixotic dream.

But there came a night when lights glowed on Howard Bay's island-stage, and the audience responded to the per-formance with fervor that stunned even the most sanguine of us. It was a phenomenon we were to grow familiar with at each performance: a sort of electricity crackling ran-domly among the audience for a time, then polarizing toward a massive discharge of emotion. Or as Mr. Marre succinctly put it, "They're not just watching a play, they're having a religious experience."

To me the most interesting aspect of the success of *Man of La Mancha* is the fact that it plows squarely upstream against the prevailing current of philosophy in the theater. That current is best identified by its catch-labels—Theater of the Absurd, Black Comedy, the Theater of Cruelty— which is to say the theater of alienation, of moral anarchy and despair. To the practitioners of those philosophies *Man of La Mancha* must seem hopelessly naïve in its espousal of illusion as man's strongest spiritual need, the most meaningful function of his imagination. But I've no unhappiness about that. "Facts are the enemy of truth," says Cervantes-Don Quixote. And that is precisely what I felt and meant.

If there was a guiding precept for the whole endeavor it lay in a quotation I found long ago in Unamuno: "Only he who attempts the absurd is capable of achieving the impossible." But on the simplest level, and philosophies aside, the play is my way of paying tribute to the tough and tender spirit of Miguel de Cervantes.

Dale Wasserman

MUSICAL NUMBERS

"Man of La Mancha" ("I, Don Quixote")	DON QUIXOTE, SANCHO AND HORSES
"It's All the Same"	ALDONZA AND MULETEERS
"Dulcinea"	DON QUIXOTE
"I'm Only Thinking of Him"	THE PADRE, ANTONIA, HOUSEKEEPER, AND DR. CARRASCO
"I Really Like Him"	SANCHO
"Little Bird, Little Bird"	ANSELMO AND MULETEERS
"Barber's Song"	THE BARBER
"Golden Helmet of Mambrino"	DON QUIXOTE, SANCHO, BARBER AND MULETEERS
"To Each His Dulcinea"	THE PADRE
"The Quest" ("The Impossible Dream")	DON QUIXOTE
"The Combat"	DON QUIXOTE, ALDONZA, SANCHO AND MULETEERS
"The Dubbing"	INNKEEPER, ALDONZA, SANCHO
"The Abduction"	ALDONZA AND MULETEERS
"Moorish Dance"	ENSEMBLE
"Aldonza"	ALDONZA
"The Knight of the Mirrors"	ENSEMBLE
"A Little Gossip"	SANCHO
"Dulcinea" (reprise)	ALDONZA
"The Quest" (reprise)	ALDONZA AND DON QUIXOTE
"Man of La Mancha" (reprise)	DON QUIXOTE, ALDONZA AND SANCHO
"The Psalm"	THE PADRE
"The Quest" (reprise)	COMPANY

MAN OF LA MANCHA

was first presented on November 22, 1965, by Albert W. Selden and Hal James at the ANTA Washington Square Theatre in New York City, with the following cast:

(IN ORDER OF APPEARANCE)

DON QUIXOTE (CERVANTES)	Richard Kiley
SANCHO (THE MANSERVANT)	Irving Jacobson
CAPTAIN OF THE INQUISITION	Renato Cibelli
ALDONZA	Joan Diener
THE INNKEEPER (THE GOVERNOR)	Ray Middleton
DR. CARRASCO (THE DUKE)	Jon Cypher
THE PADRE	Robert Rounseville
ANTONIA	Mimi Turque
THE HOUSEKEEPER	Eleanore Knapp
THE BARBER	Gino Conforti
PEDRO, HEAD MULETEER	Shev Rodgers
ANSELMO, A MULETEER	Harry Theyard
JOSE, A MULETEER	Eddie Roll
JUAN, A MULETEER	John Aristedes
PACO, A MULETEER	Antony de Vecchi
TENORIO, A MULETEER	Fernando Grahal
MARIA, THE INNKEEPER'S WIFE	Marceline Decker
FERMINA, A SERVANT GIRL	Gerrianne Raphael
THE GUITARIST	David Serva
THE HORSES	Eddie Rolland
	Fernando Grahal
GUARDS AND MEN OF THE INQUISITION	Ray Dash, Phill Lipman, Dwight Frye, John Rossi and Roger Morden

Written by Dale Wasserman

Music by Mitch Leigh

Lyrics by Joe Darion

Choreography by Jack Cole

Settings and Lighting by Howard Bay

Costumes by Howard Bay and Patton Campbell

Musical Direction and Dance Arrangements by Neil
  Warner

Musical Arrangements by Music Makers, Inc.

Book and Musical Staging by Albert Marre

Man of La Mancha

MAN OF LA MANCHA

Locale: Spain at the end of the sixteenth century. A prison in the city of Seville and various places in the imagination of MIGUEL DE CERVANTES.

Setting: The common room of a stone prison vault whose furthest reaches are lost in shadow. It has niches and crannies where the prisoners make their nests. It is below ground, reached by a stairway which may be raised and lowered, drawbridge-style, and is lighted by scant cold rays sifting through a grille overhead. A trap in the floor may be raised to permit access to a level still lower. Stage right there is a fire covered by a grille, and stage left an open well. Other scenic elements are placed and removed by the prisoners as indicated.

The prison vault is actually a single basic setting within whose architecture the DON QUIXOTE *scenes devised by* CERVANTES *play. In nature it is an abstract platform whose elements are fluid and adaptable. The primary effect is that of improvisation; it must seem as though all scenic, prop and costume items are adapted from materials already on stage, augmented by effects from* CERVANTES' *theatrical trunk.*

Only in the inner play—as devised by CERVANTES—*is there musical style and form. The prison scenes framing the inner play are not "musicalized" in the sense that there is no singing or dancing in these except as may be motivated realistically. The play is performed without intermission.*

There is an overture, then the orchestra is lost to sight as lights fade in on the common room of a prison vault. Some of the PRISONERS *lie huddled in the shadows. One*

3

strums a guitar; another dances a jaded, sensual seguiria gitana to its rhythm.

Sound and motion cease as the door at the head of the stairway opens and light streams down into the vault. The stairs are lowered and a little procession descends: first a uniformed CAPTAIN OF THE INQUISITION; *then a* SOLDIER *or two assisting a chubby* MANSERVANT *with a sizable but shabby straw trunk; then* CERVANTES *himself.*

MIGUEL DE CERVANTES *is tall and thin, a man of gentle courtliness leavened by humor. He is in his late forties but his dominant qualities are childlike—ingenuousness, a grave and endless curiosity about human behavior, candor which is very nearly self-destructive. He has, too, the child's delight in play-acting, but since he is in actuality a trained actor, when called upon to perform he translates this delight into stylish verve and gusto. On his entrance he is carrying a wrapped oblong package under one arm. It is heavy.*

CERVANTES' MANSERVANT *is as old or older than his master, short, rotund, suspicious and pragmatic. The relationship between the two is obviously of long standing; indeed, they are rather like husband and wife who bicker yet are deeply devoted.*

Now the SOLDIERS *go back up the stairs.* CERVANTES *peers about, uncertainly.*

CAPTAIN (*Watching* CERVANTES; *sardonically*) Anything wrong? The accommodations?

CERVANTES No, no, they appear quite . . . interesting.

CAPTAIN The cells are below. This is the common room, for those who wait.

CERVANTES How long do they wait?

CAPTAIN Some an hour . . . some a lifetime . . .

CERVANTES Do they all await the Inquisition?

CAPTAIN Ah, no, these are merely thieves and murderers. (*Starting to leave*) If you need anything, just shout. (*An afterthought*) If you're able.
(*He goes and the stairway is withdrawn*)

MANSERVANT (*Apprehensively*) What did he mean by that?

CERVANTES Calm yourself. There is a remedy for everything but death.

MANSERVANT That could be the very one we need!
(*The* PRISONERS *are moving, circling, approaching like animals who scent prey*)

CERVANTES (*With great courtliness*) Good morning, gentlemen . . . ladies. I regret being thrust upon you in this manner, and hope you will not find my company objectionable. In any case I shall not be among you very long. The Inquisition—
(*With a yell, the* PRISONERS *attack.* CERVANTES *and the* MANSERVANT *are seized, tripped up, pinned to the floor. The* PRISONERS *are busily rifling their pockets as* THE GOVERNOR, *a big man of obvious authority, awakens from sleep*)

THE GOVERNOR (*In a roar*) Enough! Noise, trouble, fights . . . kill each other if you must but for God's sake, do it quietly! (*To* CERVANTES) Who are you? Eh? Speak up!

CERVANTES (*Gasping as his throat is freed*) Cervantes. Don Miguel de Cervantes.

THE GOVERNOR (*With mock respect*) A gentleman!

5

CERVANTES (*Painfully getting to his feet*) It has never saved me from going to bed hungry.

THE GOVERNOR (*Indicating the* MANSERVANT) And that?

CERVANTES My servant. May I have the honor—?

THE GOVERNOR They call me The Governor. What's your game?

CERVANTES My game . . . ?

THE GOVERNOR (*Impatiently*) Your specialty, man. Cutpurse? Highwayman?

CERVANTES Oh, nothing so interesting! I am a poet.

THE DUKE (*A prisoner of draggle-tail elegance*) They're putting men in prison for that?

CERVANTES No, no, not for that.

THE DUKE (*Sardonically*) Too bad!

THE GOVERNOR (*Clapping his hands*) Well, let's get on with the trial!

CERVANTES (*As he is seized by two of the more villainous-looking* PRISONERS) Excuse me, sir. What trial?

THE GOVERNOR Yours, of course.

CERVANTES But what have I done?

THE GOVERNOR We'll find something.

CERVANTES You don't seem to understand. I'll only be here a few—

THE GOVERNOR (*Patient but firm*) My dear sir, no one

6

enters or leaves this prison without being tried by his fellow prisoners.

CERVANTES   And if I'm found guilty?

THE GOVERNOR   Oh, you will be.

CERVANTES   What sort of a sentence . . . ?

THE GOVERNOR   We generally fine a prisoner all his possessions.

CERVANTES (*Hard-hit*)   *All* of them . . .

THE GOVERNOR   Well, it's not practical to take more.

CERVANTES   One moment! These things are my livelihood.

THE GOVERNOR (*Puzzled*)   I thought you said you were a poet.

CERVANTES   Of the theater!

THE GOVERNOR (*Crossing to the trunk, digs out a sword and pulls it from its scabbard*)   False!

CERVANTES   Costumes and properties. You see, actually I am a playwright and an actor. So of course these poor things could not possibly be of any use to . . . to . . .
(*He comes to a halt, reading the inimical faces. He makes a sudden grab for the sword, but* THE GOVERNOR *tosses it over his head to another* PRISONER. *A cruel game ensues, the* PRISONERS *plundering the contents of the trunk, tossing them about as* CERVANTES *and the* MANSERVANT *stumble about, trying vainly to retrieve them*)

CERVANTES (*Panting, realizing the futility*)   Very well—take them.

7

MANSERVANT Oh, no, Master!

CERVANTES Take them, take them I say. Only leave me—
(*Clutching the package to him*)—this.
> (THE DUKE *adroitly snatches the package from him,
> tosses it to* THE GOVERNOR, *who catches it and
> weighs it in his hands*)

THE GOVERNOR Heavy! (*Shrewdly*) Valuable?

CERVANTES To me!

THE GOVERNOR We might let you ransom it.

CERVANTES I have no money.

THE GOVERNOR How unfortunate. (*Tears it open; angrily*) Paper!

CERVANTES Manuscript!

THE GOVERNOR Still worthless.
> (*He strides toward the fire with the intention of
> throwing the package in*)

CERVANTES (*Desperately*) Wait! You spoke of a trial. By
your own word, I must be given a trial!

THE GOVERNOR (*Hesitating; then peevishly*) Oh, very
well. I hereby declare this court in session! (CERVANTES
and the MANSERVANT *are shoved into an improvised
dock, and the "court" arranges itself*) Now, then. What
are you here for?

CERVANTES I am to appear before the Inquisition.
> (*There is a stir among the* PRISONERS, *one or two
> of whom cross themselves*)

THE GOVERNOR Heresy?

8

CERVANTES   Not exactly. You see, I had been employed by the government as a tax-collector . . .

THE GOVERNOR   Poet, actor, *tax-collector?*

CERVANTES   A temporary thing to keep us from starvation.

THE GOVERNOR   How does a tax-collector get in trouble with the Inquisition?

CERVANTES   I made an assessment against the monastery of La Merced. When they wouldn't pay, I issued a lien on the property.

THE GOVERNOR   You did *what?*

MANSERVANT   He foreclosed on a church.

THE GOVERNOR   But why are *you* here?

MANSERVANT (*Dolefully*)   Someone had to serve the papers.
      (*With his thumb he indicates himself*)

THE GOVERNOR   These two have empty rooms in their heads!

CERVANTES   The law says treat everyone equally. We only obeyed the law!

THE DUKE   Governor, if you don't mind, *I* should like to prosecute this case.

THE GOVERNOR   Why?

THE DUKE   Let us say I dislike stupidity. Especially when it masquerades as virtue. Miguel de Cervantes! I charge you with being an idealist, a bad poet, and an honest man. How plead you?

CERVANTES (*Considering a moment*)   Guilty.

THE GOVERNOR   Bravo!
  (*He rises, crossing toward the fire once more*)

CERVANTES   Your Excellency! What about my defense?

THE GOVERNOR (*Pausing; puzzled*)   But you just pleaded guilty.

CERVANTES (*With charm*)   Had I said "innocent" you surely would have found me guilty. Since I have admitted guilt, the court is required to hear me out.

THE GOVERNOR   For what purpose?

CERVANTES   The jury may choose to be lenient.

THE GOVERNOR   (*Thinks, then chuckles appreciatively*) Clever!

THE DUKE   He is trying to gain time!

CERVANTES   Do you have a scarcity of *that?*

THE GOVERNOR (*To the* PRISONERS)   Any urgent appointments?
  (*A groan for answer. He waves* CERVANTES *to continue*)

CERVANTES   It is true I am guilty of these charges. An idealist? Well, I have never had the courage to believe in nothing. A bad poet? This comes more painfully . . . still . . .
  (*He makes a wry gesture of acquiescence*)

THE GOVERNOR (*Skeptically*)   Have you finished your defense?

CERVANTES   Ah, no, scarce begun! If you've no objection

I should like to continue in the manner I know best . . . in the form of a charade—

THE DUKE Charade?

CERVANTES An entertainment, if you will—

THE GOVERNOR (*Intrigued*) Entertainment!

CERVANTES At worst it may beguile your time. And since my cast of characters is large, I call upon all here to enter in, to play whatever roles—

THE DUKE (*Hotly*) Governor! I should like to protest!

THE GOVERNOR No, no, let's hear him out!

CERVANTES Then . . . with your kind permission . . . may I set the stage? (THE GOVERNOR *waves assent. The* PRISONERS *shift position to become audience as* CER- VANTES *gestures to his* MANSERVANT, *who scurries, like a well-trained stage-manager, to assist. Music begins, softly, as* CERVANTES, *seated center, begins a makeup transformation as he speaks*) I shall impersonate a man . . . enter into my imagination and see him! His name is Alonso Quijana . . . a country squire, no longer young. Bony and hollow-faced . . . eyes that burn with the fire of inner vision. Being retired, he has much time for books. He studies them from morn to night, and often through the night as well. And all he reads oppresses him . . . fills him with indignation at man's murderous ways toward man. He broods . . . and broods . . . and broods—and finally from so much brooding his brains dry up! He lays down the melancholy burden of sanity and conceives the strangest project ever imagined . . . to be- come a knight-errant and sally forth into the world to right all wrongs. No longer shall he be plain Alonso

Quijana . . . but a dauntless knight known as—Don
Quixote de La Mancha!!!

> (*The* PRISONERS *giggle appreciatively as the trans-
formation of* CERVANTES *into* DON QUIXOTE *takes
place before their eyes. The* MANSERVANT, *who will
become* SANCHO PANZA, *assists with costume elements, props, and so forth*)

DON QUIXOTE (*Singing, a little tongue-in-cheek; an actor
aware that he's performing*)

> Hear me now, oh thou bleak and unbearable world!
> Thou art base and debauched as can be;
> And a knight with his banners all bravely unfurled
> Now hurls down his gauntlet to thee!
>
> I am I, Don Quixote,
> The Lord of La Mancha,
> My destiny calls and I go;
> And the wild winds of fortune will carry me onward,
> Oh whithersoever they blow.
>
> Whithersoever they blow,
> Onward to glory I go!

SANCHO

> I'm Sancho! Yes, I'm Sancho!
> I'll follow my master till the end.
> I'll tell all the world proudly
> I'm his squire! I'm his friend!

DON QUIXOTE

> Hear me, heathens and wizards and serpents of sin!
> All your dastardly doings are past;
> For a holy endeavor is now to begin,
> And virtue shall triumph at last!
>
> (*They mount the "horses"—two dancers with*

wooden frames attached—and ride away. As they
ride, the horses dance a spirited flamenco and DON
QUIXOTE *points out to* SANCHO *the sights along the*
way. They sing together)

DON QUIXOTE	SANCHO
I am I, Don Quixote,	I'm Sancho! Yes, I'm
The Lord of La Mancha,	Sancho!
My destiny calls and I go;	I'll follow my master till
And the wild winds of	the end.
fortune will carry	I'll tell all the world
me onward,	proudly
Oh whithersoever they	I'm his squire!
blow!	I'm his friend!

DON QUIXOTE and SANCHO
    Whithersoever they blow,
    Onward to glory we go!
        (*At the conclusion of the song, they dismount and*
        SANCHO *leads the "horses" to the well to drink)*

DON QUIXOTE   Well, Sancho—how dost thou like adventuring?

SANCHO   Oh, marvelous, Your Grace. But it's peculiar—to
me this great highway to glory looks exactly like the
road to El Toboso where you can buy chickens cheap.

DON QUIXOTE   Like beauty, my friend, 'tis all in the eyes
of the beholder. Only wait and thou shalt see amazing
sights.

SANCHO   What kind?

DON QUIXOTE   There will be knights and nations, warlocks, wizards . . . a cavalcade of vast, unending armies!

SANCHO   They sound dangerous!

DON QUIXOTE They *are* dangerous. But one there'll be who leads them . . . and he will be most dangerous of all!

SANCHO Well, who is he? Who?

DON QUIXOTE The Great Enchanter. Beware him, Sancho . . . for his thoughts are cold and his spirit shriveled. He has eyes like little machines, and where he walks the earth is blighted. But one day I shall meet him face to face . . . and on that day—!
(*He shakes his lance ferociously*)

SANCHO (*Sensibly*) Well, I wouldn't get upset, Your Grace. As I always say, have patience and shuffle the cards.

DON QUIXOTE Do you never run out of proverbs?

SANCHO No, Your Grace. I was born with a bellyful of them. I always say—

DON QUIXOTE (*Looking off as the projected shadows of a great windmill's sails cross the stage*) Aah-hah!

SANCHO What is it?

DON QUIXOTE How long since we sallied forth?

SANCHO About two minutes?

DON QUIXOTE So soon shall I engage in brave, unequal combat!

SANCHO Combat? Where?

DON QUIXOTE Can'st not see? (*Pointing*) A monstrous giant of infamous repute!

SANCHO (*Looking vainly; the "horses" are interested, too*) *What* giant?

14

Joan Diener and Richard Kiley, as ALDONZA and DON QUIXOTE, talk in the courtyard of the inn.

DON QUIXOTE
>It is that dark and dreaded ogre
>By the name of Matagoger!
>You can tell him by the four great arms awhirling on
>   his back!

SANCHO   It's a windmill.

DON QUIXOTE (*Shouting*)
>Ho! Feckless giant standing there!
>Avast! Avaunt! On guard! Beware!
>   (*He charges off*)

SANCHO   No, no, Your Grace, I swear by my wife's little black mustache, that's not a giant, it's only a—
(*Offstage a crash; the horses run for cover. To musical
accompaniment the combat continues as* SANCHO *dances
about, dodging first* QUIXOTE'S *helmet which comes flying
back onstage, then the butt of his lance, splayed and
splintered. The final crash; and* QUIXOTE *crawls back into
view, his sword a corkscrew. A doleful picture, he comes
rolling downstage as* SANCHO *hurries to plump himself
down and stop him*) Didn't I tell you? Didn't I say,
"Your Grace, that's a windmill"?

DON QUIXOTE (*Hollowly*)   The work of my enemy.

SANCHO   The Enchanter?

DON QUIXOTE   He changed that giant into a windmill at
the last moment. He will take any advantage in order
to— (*A pause; an illumination*) Sancho, it comes to me!

SANCHO   What, Your Grace?

DON QUIXOTE   How he was able to upset me. It is because
I have never properly been dubbed a knight.

SANCHO That's no problem. Just tell me how it's done and I'll be glad to take care of this drubbing.

DON QUIXOTE Dubbing. Thank you, my friend, but it may only be done by another knight.

SANCHO (*Dismayed*) *That's* a problem. I've never *seen* another knight.

DON QUIXOTE The lord of some castle would do. Or a king or a duke.

SANCHO (*Helping* QUIXOTE *to his feet*) Very well. I'll keep an eye out for any kings or dukes as we go.

DON QUIXOTE (*Looking off*) Ahaaa!

SANCHO (*Apprehensively*) Now what?

DON QUIXOTE The very place!

SANCHO Where?

DON QUIXOTE There!

SANCHO If Your Grace would just give me a hint . . . ?

DON QUIXOTE There in the distance. A castle!

SANCHO (*Peering vainly*) Castle.

DON QUIXOTE Rockbound amidst the crags!

SANCHO Crags.

DON QUIXOTE And the banners—ah, the brave banners flaunting in the wind!

SANCHO Anything on 'em?

DON QUIXOTE (*Shielding his eyes*) I see a cat crouching on a field tawny . . . and beneath it the inscription "Miau"!

SANCHO Oh, that's fine, Your Grace. Maybe this is where you can get yourself drubbed.

DON QUIXOTE Dubbed. (*Excitedly*) Blow thy bugle that a dwarf may mount the battlements and announce our coming!

SANCHO (*Under the spell, lifts his bugle then hesitates*) But I don't *see* a castle. I do see something . . . maybe it's an inn.

DON QUIXOTE (*Sadly*) An inn.

SANCHO We'd better pass it by, Your Grace. Those roadside places are full of rough men and women.

DON QUIXOTE Come. We shall ride straight to the drawbridge of yon castle, and there thy vision may improve!
    (*The lights fade to transition lighting as* QUIXOTE *and* SANCHO *drop out of character.*

    CERVANTES *beckons to the* PRISONERS *who will become* MULETEERS *in the next scene; they and the* SERVANT *proceed to set up the Great Room of an inn as he speaks*)

CERVANTES Here is an example of how to the untrained eye one thing may seem to be another. To Sancho, an inn. To Quixote, a castle. To someone else, whatever his mind may make of it. But for the sake of argument, let us grant Sancho *his* vision. An inn . . . (*He gestures to* THE GOVERNOR—*then to a lady prisoner*) A kindly innkeeper . . . his less kindly wife . . . (*He picks out some of the other* PRISONERS) Rough men—muleteers—fifteen miles on the road today. Rough women—in most particular a woman called—Aldonza!

MULETEERS (*Making a chant of her name, banging their tin dishes on the table*) Aldonza, Aldonza, Aldonza! (*A pan comes sailing in; the men dodge it to prevent being hit.* ALDONZA *enters; a savage, dark alley-cat, survivor if not always victor of many back-fence tussles*)

ALDONZA (*With a pot of stew in her hands; roughly*) You want it on the table or over your lousy heads? (*The* MULETEERS *laugh. She sets down the tureen with a crash, and spits into it*)

ALDONZA There, swine. Feed! (*She starts to distribute goatskins of wine. The* MULETEERS, *of whom there are seven, are variously called* JOSE, TENORIO, PACO, JUAN, ANSELMO *and* PEDRO. *The seventh, nameless, is the prisoner with the guitar.* JOSE *is the runt of the gang;* PEDRO, *the biggest, is its leader*)

JOSE (*Amorously*) I brought you something.

ALDONZA Keep it till it grows up. (PACO *whispers in her ear*) Little dogs have big ideas!

JUAN Tonight?

ALDONZA Payment in advance? (*He gets on his knees wanting her to pour the wine into his mouth; she pours it onto his head*)

PEDRO (*Laughing*) Aldonza! Sweetheart. Come here.

ALDONZA Talk with your mouth, not your hands!

PEDRO (*Pulling her close; confidentially*) I've got a nice thick bed of hay in the stable.

ALDONZA (*As confidentially*)   Good. Eat it.

PEDRO   You would refuse Pedro?

ALDONZA   Try me.
   (*She walks away from him*)

PEDRO   My *mules* are not as stubborn!
   (*He snaps his whip at her*)

ALDONZA   Fine! Make love to your mules!
   (*The* MULETEERS *laugh, then sing*)

MULETEERS
   I come for love,
   I come for love,
   I come to Aldonza for love!

ALDONZA (*Contemptuously*)   Love! (*She sings*)
   One pair of arms is like another,
   I don't know why or who's to blame,
   I'll go with you or with your brother,
   It's all the same, it's all the same!

   This I have learned: that when the light's out,
   No man will burn with special flame,
   You'll prove to me, before the night's out,
   You're all the same, you're all the same!

   So do not talk to me of love,
   I'm not a fool with starry eyes,
   Just put your money in my hand,
   And you will get what money buys!

   One pair of arms is like another,
   I don't know why or who's to blame,
   I'll go with you or with your brother,
   It's all the same, it's all the same!

(*The* MULETEERS *reach for her, roughly; she pushes them off*)

Oh, I have seen too many beds,
But I have known too little rest,
And I have loved too many men
With hatred burning in my breast.

I do not like you or your brother,
I do not like the life I live,
But I am me, I am Aldonza,
And what I give I choose to give!

> (PEDRO *offers money to* ALDONZA, *throws it on the floor. She spits on it and backs away, luring him. He follows and presses the money into her hand*)

One pair of arms . . . is like another
It's all the same, it's all the same!

> (*She exits*)

ANSELMO (*Laughing*)   Payment before delivery?

PACO   She won't deliver.

PEDRO   She'll deliver!

> (*The* INNKEEPER *enters with his wife,* MARIA, *and another serving-girl,* FERMINA)

INNKEEPER   Well gentlemen, everything in order?

> (*He surveys the interior of his inn which is somewhat the worse for wear after the violence of the preceding number.* MARIA *and* FERMINA *begin to clean up*)

ANSELMO   Did you feed the mules?

INNKEEPER   They're eating as well as you.

20

PEDRO God forbid!

INNKEEPER He jokes! It's well known that I set the finest table between Madrid and Malaga. My patrons have always—
> (*From offstage there comes the blast of a bugle horribly blown*)

PEDRO What in the name of—?
> (*The bugle sounds again*)

INNKEEPER (*His face lighting up*) The pig-butcher! I didn't expect him till tomorrow. (*Hurrying to the door*) Coming, Señor Butcher, coming!
> (*He stops short as* DON QUIXOTE *and* SANCHO *enter.* QUIXOTE *has replaced his lance with the limb of a tree*)

DON QUIXOTE (*Haughtily*) Is the lord of the castle at hand? (*No reply from the flabbergasted* INNKEEPER) I say, is the Castellano here?

INNKEEPER (*With an effort*) I am in charge of this place.

DON QUIXOTE (*Coldly*) We waited, sire, for a dwarf to mount the battlements and announce us, but none appeared.

INNKEEPER The . . . the dwarfs are all busy.
> (QUIXOTE *makes a haughty signal to* SANCHO, *who delivers himself of a rehearsed speech*)

SANCHO Noble lords and ladies. My master, Don Quixote, knight-errant and defender of the right and pursuer of lofty undertakings, implores the boon of hospitality!
> (*The* INNKEEPER *looks open-mouthed at the* MULE-TEERS, *who look back in kind*)

21

DON QUIXOTE Well, sir? Is it granted?

INNKEEPER (*Pulling himself together*) Absolutely! This inn—I mean, this castle—is open to everybody.

MARIA (*To the* INNKEEPER, *frightened*) A madman!

INNKEEPER (*Aside, to* MARIA) Madmen are the children of God. (*To* QUIXOTE) Sir knight, you must be hungry.

DON QUIXOTE Aye, that I am.

INNKEEPER There's food aplenty, and for your squire, too. I'll just help him stable your animals.
        (*He motions to* SANCHO *to follow, and they exit*)

DON QUIXOTE (*Approaching the others*) Gentle knights! Fair chatelaine! If there be any among you that require assistance, you have but to speak and my good right arm is at your service. Whether it be a princess held for ransom, an army besieged and awaiting rescue, or merely . . . (ALDONZA *has emerged laden with things for the table. She stops, puzzled at the silence.* DON QUIXOTE *is gazing at her, stricken*) Dear God . . . it is she! (ALDONZA *stares. He averts his eyes worshipfully*) Sweet lady . . . fair virgin . . . I dare not gaze full upon thy countenance lest I be blinded by beauty. But I implore thee—speak once thy name.

ALDONZA (*A growl*) Aldonza.

DON QUIXOTE My lady jests.

ALDONZA Aldonza!

DON QUIXOTE (*Approaching her*) The name of a kitchen-scullion . . . or mayhap my lady's serving-maid?

ALDONZA I told you my name! Now get out of the way, or I'll—

DON QUIXOTE (*Smiling*) Did my lady think to put me to a test? Ah, sweet sovereign of my captive heart, I shall not fail thee, for I *know*. (*Singing*)
> I have dreamed thee too long,
> Never seen thee or touched thee, but known thee
>   with all of my heart,
> Half a prayer, half a song,
> Thou hast always been with me, though we have been
>   always apart.
>
> Dulcinea . . . Dulcinea . . .
> I see heaven when I see thee, Dulcinea,
> And thy name is like a prayer an angel whispers . . .
> Dulcinea . . . Dulcinea!
>
> If I reach out to thee,
> Do not tremble and shrink from the touch of my hand
>   on thy hair.
> Let my fingers but see
> Thou art warm and alive, and no phantom to fade in
>   the air.
>
> Dulcinea . . . Dulcinea . . .
> I have sought thee, sung thee, dreamed thee, Dulcinea!
> Now I've found thee, and the world shall know thy
>   glory.
> Dulcinea . . . Dulcinea!

INNKEEPER (*Entering; to* QUIXOTE) Come along, Señor Knight! I'll show you to your quarters.
> (*He maneuvers* QUIXOTE *offstage*)

MARIA (*Mocking, to* ALDONZA) Ay, Dulcinea!
> (*The* MULETEERS *launch into an elaborate parody of the song*)

23

MULETEERS (*Singing*)
> Dulcinea . . . Dulcinea . . .
> I see heaven when I see thee, Dulcinea.

ANSELMO
> And thy name is like a prayer an angel whispers . . .
> Dulcinea . . . Dulcinea . . .

MULETEERS
> Dulcinea . . . Dulcinea . . .
> I have sought thee, sung thee, dreamed thee, Dulcinea!
> Now I've found thee, and the world shall know thy glory,
> Dulcinea . . . Dulcinea!
>> (*By the end* ALDONZA *has driven them about the stage, belaboring them in fury—as the lighting changes back to the prison.* THE DUKE *is in the center of the arena, shouting the others down*)

THE DUKE   Governor! Governor! If you don't mind—this man proposed to offer a defense!

CERVANTES   This *is* my defense.

THE DUKE   The most curious I've ever heard!

CERVANTES   But if it entertains . . . ?

THE DUKE (*Waspishly*)   The word is "diverts." I think *your* purpose is to divert us from *ours.*

CERVANTES (*Cheerfully*)   Precisely! And now if I may get on with it . . . ?

THE GOVERNOR   Continue your defense!
>> (CERVANTES, *again the scene-master, selects people and arranges the next sequence as he speaks*)

CERVANTES Imagine now the family our brave knight left behind! Not the lords and ladies and retainers of Don Quixote de La Mancha, but the simple womenfolk of a country squire known as Alonso Quijana. (*A musical underscore begins as he beckons to three of the* PRISONERS, *handing them costumes*) Imagine their shock as news of the master's madness reaches them! To his niece, Antonia—who is worried about its effect on her forthcoming marriage. To his housekeeper of many years—who is worried about even darker matters. To the local Padre who has known Alonso all of his life. (*To* THE DUKE) And shortly there will enter a character whose philosophy may appeal—enormously—to you! (*He slings a costume to* THE DUKE) Alonso's niece and his housekeeper hurry to the neighborhood church. (*To his* MAN-SERVANT) May we have a church, please? Anguished by this terrible situation—and not unaware of what the neighbors may think—they seek help and advice from the Padre. (*The* PRISONER *selected for the* PADRE, *now costumed, giggles with delight in his role.* CERVANTES *wipes the smile from his face, adjusts his posture*) The Padre. (*The* PRISONER *composes himself instantly, walks into the scene. Setting and lighting have changed; we are now in a simple country church. There are confessional screens left and right. The* PADRE *is between, listening alternately to the plaints of the two women beyond their respective screens where* CERVANTES *has positioned them, puppet-like*) But in spite of the trouble which the Squire's madness may bring down upon *their* heads, you may be sure they are only thinking of him!

(*He snaps his fingers, and the people come to life, singing*)

ANTONIA

I'm only thinking of him,
I'm only thinking of him,
Whatever I may do or say,
I'm only thinking of him!
In my body, it's well known,
There is not one selfish bone—
I'm only thinking and worrying about him!

I've been told he's chasing dragons and I fear it may
be true.
If my groom should hear about it, heaven knows what
he will do!
Oh, I dearly love my uncle but for what he's done
to me
I would like to take and lock him up and throw away
the key!

But if I do . . .
But if I do . . .
There is one thing that I swear will still be true . . .

ANTONIA and   PADRE
  HOUSEKEEPER

ANTONIA and HOUSEKEEPER	PADRE
I'm only thinking of him;	I know, I know, my dear,
I'm only thinking of him;	Of course you are, my dear;
I'm only thinking and worrying about him.	I understand.

HOUSEKEEPER

    Oh, I think he's been too lonely, living years without
        a spouse,
    So when he returns I fear I may have trouble in the
        house;
    For they say he seeks a lady, who his own true love
        shall be;
    God forbid that in his madness he should ever think
        it's me!
      (*The* PADRE *steals a look around the screen at her,*
      incredulously)
    If he should try
    I'll surely die,
    And I will grimly guard my honor as I cry—

HOUSEKEEPER	PADRE	ANTONIA
I'm only think-ing of him;	I know, I know, my dear;	(*Her wail continues throughout*)
I'm only think-ing of him;	Of course you are, my dear;	Woe, woe, woe . . .
I'm only think-ing and wor-rying about him.	I understand.	

HOUSEKEEPER

    Woe!

      (*Her wail makes the* PADRE *wince and recoil to-*
      ward ANTONIA)

ANTONIA

    Woe!

      (*The* PADRE *winces and recoils in the other direc-*
      tion)

PADRE	HOUSEKEEPER	ANTONIA
(Slipping to his knees; addressing God)	Woe, woe . . .	Woe, woe . . .

They're only thinking
   of him,
They're only thinking
   of him,
How saintly is their
   plaintive plea—
They're only thinking
   of him!
What a comfort, to be
   sure
That their motives are
   so pure—
As they go thinking and
   worrying about him!

> (CERVANTES *appears in the lights, ushering forward* THE DUKE, *now dressed in academic cap and gown*)

CERVANTES   And now there appears on the scene a man of breeding . . . intelligence . . . logic. He is Antonia's fiancé, Doctor Sansón Carrasco—Bachelor of Science—graduate of the University of Salamanca! (*Drily*) A man who carries his own self-importance as though afraid of breaking it. (*Places* CARRASCO *in one corner of the stage. The quartet immediately starts arguing.* CERVANTES *claps his hands for silence*) I had forgotten that family quarrels have a way of getting out of hand. With so much at stake in the game, let us rearrange the pieces! (*Moving* ANTONIA *to a second corner*) The queen—cunning! (*Moving the* HOUSEKEEPER *to a third corner*) The castle—formidable! (*Moving the* PADRE *to the fourth corner*) The bishop—charmingly diagonal! (*Sitting center*) And now—the problem of the knight!

ANTONIA Sansón!

PADRE Have you heard?

DR. CARRASCO On my way here I was informed by at least ten people. (*To* ANTONIA) My dear, your uncle is the laughingstock of the entire neighborhood. Padre? What do you know of this?

PADRE Only that the good Señor Quijana has been carried away by his imagination.

DR. CARRASCO Señor Quijana has lost his mind and is suffering from delusions.

PADRE Is there a difference?

DR. CARRASCO Exactitude of meaning. I beg to remind you, Padre, that I am a doctor.

ANTONIA Please don't argue, we must *do* something about him!

DR. CARRASCO I'm a little more concerned about *us*.

ANTONIA What do you mean, us?

DR. CARRASCO Our marriage, my dear. There is a certain embarrassment at having a madman in the family. In the eyes of others—

PADRE (*Alarmed at this drift*) Oh, come, come, Doctor.

DR. CARRASCO I do not relish claiming a lunatic as uncle!

29

HOUSEKEEPER (*Nodding, a sibyl*) The innocent must pay for the sins of the guilty.

PADRE Guilty of what? A gentle delusion!

DR. CARRASCO How do you know it is gentle? By this time who knows what violence he has committed! He was armed?

HOUSEKEEPER With sword and lance.
(CARRASCO *throws up his hands*)

ANTONIA (*Voice forlorn, wistful*) Sansón. I had hoped for so much for us. For *you*, really. Everything was to be for you. My uncle's house . . . his lands . . .

PADRE (*The devil's advocate*) True, Doctor. In time they would all be yours. After all, if one is to serve science, one must have the means.

DR. CARRASCO (*Outraged*) Are you priest or pawnbroker?

PADRE (*Swiftly revising his approach*) What I meant was—consider the challenge.

DR. CARRASCO Challenge?

PADRE Think what cleverness it would take to wean this man from madness. To turn him from his course and persuade him to return home.
(CERVANTES *rises: clever approach*)

DR. CARRASCO (*Pondering*) Hmmm . . . that *is* a challenge.

PADRE Impossible.

DR. CARRASCO He can't have gotten far?

PADRE No more than a day's journey!

DR. CARRASCO   Get ready, Padre. We shall go after him.
(*As they prepare to leave, the* DOCTOR *sings*)
But as we go . . .
But as we go . . .
There is one thing that I want the world to know!

PADRE (*Singing, aside*)
I feel, with pain,
That once again,
We now will hear a very often heard refrain.
(*They sing in chorus*)

DR. CARRASCO   PADRE
I'm only thinking of him—   He's only thinking of him,

ANTONIA and HOUSEKEEPER
You're only thinking of   He's only thinking of him,
    him—   just him.

ANTONIA, HOUSEKEEPER and DR. CARRASCO
Whatever we may do or say,
We're only thinking of him.

In our bodies it's well known
There is not one selfish bone . . .

ANTONIA, HOUSEKEEPER   PADRE
and DR. CARRASCO
We're only thinking and   They're only thinking and
    worrying about him!   worrying about him!

(*Lights dim out on them as* CERVANTES, *isolated
in his own light, steps forward*)

CERVANTES   Let us return now to the inn. To the *kitchen*
of the inn. A kitchen, ladies, if you please? Thank you.
(*Taking the pots, sniffing as he places them*) Ah yes,
tomorrow's onion stew. Chicken tripes, with . . . pep-

31

per. Now then! As everyone knows, it is imperative that each knight shall have a lady—for a knight without a lady is like a body without a soul. To whom would he dedicate his conquests? What vision sustain him when he sallies forth to do battle with ogres and with giants? (*He points to the stage area where lights come up on* ALDONZA, *seated in what is now the kitchen, gobbling her supper.* SANCHO *is seen approaching.* CERVANTES *hands him a sheet of paper*) Don Quixote, having discovered his lady, sends his faithful squire to her with a missive.

(*The transition is complete;* CERVANTES *exits*)

ALDONZA (*To* SANCHO, *suspiciously*) Missive? What's a missive?

SANCHO   A sort of a letter. He warned me to give it only into your hand.

ALDONZA (*Darkly*) Let's see it. (*She takes the rolled sheet from* SANCHO, *inspects both sides. Sullenly*) I can't read.

SANCHO   Neither can I. But my master, foreseeing such a possibility, recited it to me so I could commit it to heart.

ALDONZA (*Angrily*) What made him think I couldn't read?

SANCHO   Well, as he explained it, noblewomen are so busy with their needlework—

ALDONZA   *Needlework?*

SANCHO   Embroidering banners for their knights. He said they had no time for study.

ALDONZA (*Contemptuously*) What's it say?
      (SANCHO *takes the letter from her, holds it before*

him, and closes his eyes. Music: the quotations from the letter are sung. All other lines are spoken)

SANCHO
"Most lovely sovereign and highborn lady—"

ALDONZA (*Continuing to gobble her supper*) Ho.

SANCHO
"The heart of this, thy vassal knight, faints for thy favor."

ALDONZA Ha.

SANCHO
"Oh, fairest of the fair, purest of the pure; Incomparable Dulcinea—"

ALDONZA *That* again. My name is Aldonza!

SANCHO (*Patiently*) My master calls you Dulcinea.

ALDONZA (*Glowering*) Why?

SANCHO I don't know, but I can tell you from experience that knights have their own language for everything, and it's better not to ask questions because it only gets you into trouble. (ALDONZA *makes a contemptuous gesture for him to continue*)
"I beg thee grant that I may kiss the nethermost hem of thy garment—"

ALDONZA Kiss my *which?*

SANCHO If you keep interrupting, the whole thing will be gone out of my head!

ALDONZA Well, what's he *want?*

SANCHO I'm getting to it!
"—And send to me a token of thy fair esteem that I may carry as my standard into battle."

33

ALDONZA What kind of a token?

SANCHO He says generally it's a silken scarf.

ALDONZA Your master's a crackbrain!

SANCHO Oh, no!

ALDONZA (*Mimicking*) Oh, yes!

SANCHO Well, they say one madman makes a hundred and love makes a thousand.

ALDONZA What's that mean?

SANCHO I'm not sure.

ALDONZA You're crazy, too! (*A pause*) Well, what are you waiting for?

SANCHO (*Patiently*) The token.

ALDONZA I'll give him a token. Here!
(*She flings him the filthy, tattered dishcloth she has been using*)

SANCHO (*Examining it in dismay*) But my lady—

ALDONZA Don't you "my lady" me too or I'll crack you like an egg! (SANCHO *retreats*) Wait a minute. Come here. Sit. *Sit!* (*She pats the stool and* SANCHO *sits, she beside him on the floor*) Tell me—why do you follow him?

SANCHO Well, that's easy to explain, I . . . I . . .
(*The reason seems to elude him*)

ALDONZA Why?

SANCHO I'm *telling* you. It's because . . . because . . .

ALDONZA *Why?*

34

SANCHO (*Giving up; simply, he sings*)
    I like him.
    I really like him.
    Tear out my fingernails one by one, I like him!

    I don't have
    A very good reason.
    Since I've been with him cuckoonuts have been in
        season—

    But there's nothing I can do,
    Chop me up for onion stew,
    Still I'll yell to the sky,
    Though I can't tell you why,
    That I like him!

ALDONZA It doesn't make any sense!

SANCHO That's because you're not a squire.

ALDONZA All right, you're a squire. How does a squire squire?

SANCHO Well, I ride behind him . . . and he fights. Then I pick him up off the ground . . .

ALDONZA But what do *you* get out of it?

SANCHO What do *I* get? Plenty! Why, already I've gotten . . .

ALDONZA You've gotten nothing! So why do you *do* it?

SANCHO (*Sings*)
    I like him.
    I really like him.
    Pluck me naked as a scalded chicken, I like him!

35

Don't ask me
For why or wherefore,
'Cause I don't have a single good "Because" or "There-
      fore."

You can barbecue my nose,
Make a giblet of my toes,
Make me freeze, make me fry,
Make me sigh, make me cry,
Still I'll yell to the sky
Though I can't tell you why,
That I . . . like . . . him!

> (*He exits, in his own kind of dignity, leaving* AL-
> DONZA *puzzled and less sure.*
>
> *A cross-dim in the lighting, out on the kitchen;
> up the well stage left where* CERVANTES *is entering
> with the* MULETEERS, *prompting them in the next
> song they are to sing. Night lighting; the mood
> lyric, sentimental. Satisfied that they are singing it
> properly,* CERVANTES *exits, and the* MULETEERS,
> *lounging about the coping of the well, swell into
> full harmony to the guitarist's accompaniment*)

MULETEERS (*During this,* ALDONZA *picks up a bucket and
crosses the courtyard to the well. Lights will fade out
in the kitchen. As* ALDONZA *approaches, the lines sung
by the* MULETEERS *have focused upon her with mocking,
though light-hearted double-entendre. She pushes one or
two of them out of the way in order to get to the well.
They sing the last lines of the song to her legs*)

> Little bird, little bird,
> In the cinnamon tree,
> Little bird, little bird,
> Do you sing for me?

Do you bring me word
Of one I know?
Little bird, little bird, I love her so,
Little bird, little bird, I have to know,
Little bird, little bird.

Beneath this tree, this cinnamon tree,
We learned to love, we learned to cry;
For here we met and here we kissed,
And here one cold and moonless night we said
    goodbye.

Little bird, little bird,
Oh have pity on me,
Bring her back to me now
'Neath the cinnamon tree.

I have waited too long
Without a song . . .
Little bird, little bird, please fly, please go,
Little bird, little bird, and tell her so,
Little bird, little bird!

ALDONZA (*Dispassionately*) I spit in the milk of your
"little bird."
    (*She bends over to fill the bucket from the well.
    PEDRO spies the letter*)

PEDRO Here, what's this?
    (*He snatches it*)

ALDONZA Give it back!

PEDRO (*Fending her off*) It's a letter.

ALDONZA That shows how stupid you are; it's a missive!

PEDRO *Missive?* (*Holding it up*) Who reads?

(ANSELMO *holds up a hand.* PEDRO *tosses him the letter.* ALDONZA *would try to retrieve it but is held by* PEDRO *and another of the* MULETEERS)

PEDRO (*Reprovingly, closing her mouth with a hand*) Sh-h-h!

ALDONZA Sons of whores!
(*She bites him*)

ANSELMO (*Haltingly, mispronouncing words*) "Most lovely sovereign and highborn lady—!" It's from her knight. A love letter!

ALDONZA A stupid joke!

TENORIO Then why so hot about it?

PEDRO Has he touched your heart?

ALDONZA Nobody touches *my* heart.

ANSELMO All these fine words . . . !

ALDONZA (*Snatching back the letter*) Fine words. He's a man, isn't he? All right, he wants what every other man wants.
(*She picks up her buckets of water and starts off.* PEDRO *stops her*)

PEDRO Hey, Aldonza . . . now?

ALDONZA (*Sullenly*) Later . . . when I'm through in the kitchen.
(*She exits. The* MULETEERS *continue singing softly as the* PADRE *and* DR. CARRASCO *enter.* FERMINA *enters and crosses to them. They indicate in pantomime that she bring* DON QUIXOTE *to them. She exits*)

PADRE   I confess I shall not know what to say to him.

DR. CARRASCO   In that case, leave it to me.

PADRE   He may not even know us!

DR. CARRASCO   I am prepared for that contingency. Should
he fail to recognize us . . .
    (*He is interrupted*)

DON QUIXOTE (*From offstage; he enters during the course
of his speech*)   Who is it crieth help of Don Quixote
de La Mancha? Is there a castle beleaguered by giants?
A king who lies under enchantment? An army besieged
and awaiting rescue? (*Surprised, he advances toward
them*) Why, what is this? (*With cordial welcome*) My
friends!

DR. CARRASCO (*Taken aback*)   You know us?

DON QUIXOTE (*Equally puzzled*)   Should a man not know
his friends, Dr. Carrasco? (*With great warmth, taking
his hand*)—Padre Perez!

PADRE (*In deep relief*)   Ah, Señor Quijana—

DON QUIXOTE (*In cool reproof*)   I should prefer that you
address me properly. I am Don Quixote, knight-errant
of La Mancha.
    (*The* PADRE *quails and sinks to a seat*)

DR. CARRASCO   Señor Quijana—

DON QUIXOTE   Don Quixote.

DR. CARRASCO   There are no giants. No kings under enchantment. No chivalry. No knights. There have been
no knights for three hundred years.

39

DON QUIXOTE (*To the* PADRE, *pityingly*)   So learned, yet so misinformed.

DR. CARRASCO   These are *facts*.

DON QUIXOTE   Facts are the enemy of truth.

SANCHO (*Entering*)   Your Grace—

DON QUIXOTE (*Eagerly*)   Well? Did she receive thee? (SANCHO *nods*) Ah, most fortunate of squires! The token. What of the token? (SANCHO *proffers the ragged dishcloth.* QUIXOTE *takes it with reverence*) Sheer gossamer. (*Turning away*) Forgive me. I am overcome.

SANCHO (*To the* PADRE *and* CARRASCO, *confidentially*)   It's from his lady.

DR. CARRASCO (*Pouncing*)   So there's a woman!

DON QUIXOTE   A *lady!* (*Softening*) The lady Dulcinea. Her beauty is more than human. Her quality? Perfection. She is the very meaning of woman . . . and all meaning woman has to man.

PADRE (*With a sad smile*)   To each his Dulcinea.
      (*A happy caroling is heard from someone approaching the inn*)

DON QUIXOTE (*Hearing and turning*)   Someone approaches . . . !

SANCHO   It's just an ordinary traveler.

DON QUIXOTE   But see what he wears upon his head! Get thee to a place of hiding, Sancho.

SANCHO (*Apprehensively*)   Oh, dear!
      (*He hides as* QUIXOTE *too conceals himself to one side*)

BARBER (*Singing offstage*)
>Oh, I am a little barber
>And I go my merry way,
>With my razor and my leeches
>I can always earn my pay.

>Though your chin be smooth as satin,
>You will need me soon I know,
>For the Lord protects His barbers,
>And He makes the stubble grow.

BARBER (*Enters. He carries a bundle of equipment, and on his head is wearing a brass shaving basin. He sings to the* MULETEERS)
>If I slip when I am shaving you
>And cut you to the quick,
>You can use me as a doctor,
>'Cause I also heal the sick.
>>(QUIXOTE *comes up behind him and prods him with his sword. The* BARBER *turns, unbelieving*)

By the beard of St. Anthony—I could swear I see before me a knight in full armor! (*He chuckles*) Ridiculous. There aren't any knights. (QUIXOTE *roars, raising his sword. The* BARBER *falls to his knees*) I was wrong! Forgive me, Your Highness, I thought I'd been touched by the sun!

DON QUIXOTE Thou wilt be touched by worse if thou dost not speedily hand over that Golden Helmet!

BARBER Golden helmet? What? Where? (*Takes the basin off, examines it*) Why, this is nothing but a shaving basin!

DON QUIXOTE (*With fine contempt*) Shaving basin.

SANCHO (*Examining it*)   I must say, Your Grace, it *does* look like a shaving basin.

BARBER (*Eagerly*)   Of course! You see, I am a barber. A barber? I ply my trade from village to village, and I was wearing this on my head to ward off the rays of the sun, so that's how Your Highship made the mistake of—

DON QUIXOTE   Silence! (*The* BARBER *flinches and is silent. Impressively, to* CARRASCO *and the* PADRE) Know thou what that really is? The Golden Helmet of Mambrino! When worn by one of noble heart it renders him invulnerable to all wounds! (*To the* BARBER) Misbegotten knave—where didst thou steal it?

BARBER   I didn't steal it!

DON QUIXOTE   Hand it over.

BARBER   But it cost me half a crown!

DON QUIXOTE   Hand it over or I shall—!
    (*He takes a mighty swipe with his sword. The* BARBER *yelps and tumbles out of the way, abandoning the basin which* SANCHO *catches*)

SANCHO (*With satisfaction*)   It *is* worth half a crown.

DON QUIXOTE   Fool! (*His face lights up; he tosses away his old casque, handling the basin with reverence and pleasure. He sings*)
    Thou Golden Helmet of Mambrino,
    With so illustrious a past,
    Too long hast thou been lost to glory,
    Th'art rediscovered now at last!

Golden Helmet of Mambrino,
There can be no
Hat like thee!

Thee and I, now,
'Ere I die, now,
Will make golden
History!

BARBER

I can hear the cuckoo singing
in the cuckooberry tree . . .

SANCHO

If he says that that's a helmet, I suggest
that you agree . . .

BARBER

But he'll find it is not gold and will not
make him bold and brave . . .

SANCHO

Well, at least he'll find it useful if he ever
needs a shave!

(SANCHO *and the* BARBER *move toward* QUIXOTE *who has indicated that the* PADRE *should "crown" him with the golden helmet as he kneels. Just as* QUIXOTE *is about to be crowned, he remembers the token, takes it from inside his tunic and hands it to* SANCHO *indicating that it be attached to the helmet before the crowning is completed.* SANCHO *does so, handing the helmet back to the* PADRE *who completes the coronation. All this has happened to the amazement of the* MULETEERS, *the utter disbelief of the* BARBER, *and the worshipful attendance of* SANCHO)

43

DON QUIXOTE
>   Thou Golden Helmet of Mambrino,
>   Thy deeds the world will not forget;
>   Now Don Quixote de La Mancha
>   Will bring thee greater glory yet!

>   Golden—

DON QUIXOTE	THE OTHERS
—Helmet of Mambrino	—Helmet of Mambrino,
There can be no	There can be no
Hat like thee!	Hat like thee!
Thee and I, now,	Thee and he now,
'Ere I die now	We can see, now
Will make golden	Will make golden
History!	History!

>   (SANCHO *slowly drags the astounded* BARBER *off
>   and away from* QUIXOTE, *as the* MULETEERS, *one
>   of them sobbing uncontrollably at the amazing
>   sight, drift off. The* PADRE *and* DR. CARRASCO, *apparently giving up their mission, also leave. Lights
>   dim down and the* INNKEEPER *enters*)

INNKEEPER (*Surprised to find* QUIXOTE *alone*) Your friends have departed?

DON QUIXOTE (*Turning on his knees*) Sir Castellano—I would make a confession.

INNKEEPER To me?

DON QUIXOTE I would confess that I have never actually been dubbed a knight.

INNKEEPER Oh. That's bad!

DON QUIXOTE And yet I am well qualified, my lord. I am brave, courteous, bold, generous, affable and patient.

44

INNKEEPER (*Judiciously*) Yes . . . that's the list.

DON QUIXOTE Therefore I would beg a boon of thee.

INNKEEPER Anything! Within reason.

DON QUIXOTE Tonight I would hold vigil in the chapel of thy castle, and at dawn receive from thy hand the ennobling stroke of knighthood.

INNKEEPER Hmm. There's one small difficulty. No chapel.

DON QUIXOTE What?

INNKEEPER (*Hastily*) That is—it's being repaired. But if you wouldn't mind holding your vigil someplace else . . . ?

DON QUIXOTE (*A happy thought*) Here in the courtyard. Under the stars . . . !

INNKEEPER Fine! At sunrise you'll be dubbed a knight.

DON QUIXOTE I thank thee.

INNKEEPER *Now* will you have some supper?

DON QUIXOTE Supper? Before a vigil? Nay, my lord, on this night I must fast and compose my spirit.
> (*He and the* INNKEEPER *exit separately as the lights pick up the* PADRE *and* CARRASCO)

PADRE There is either the wisest madman or the maddest wise man in the world.

DR. CARRASCO He is mad.

PADRE Well . . . in any case we have failed.

DR. CARRASCO (*Tightly*) Not necessarily. We know the sickness. Now to find the cure.
> (*He exits*)

45

PADRE (*Reflecting for a moment*) The cure. May it be
not worse than the disease. (*Music: as he sings we will
see* QUIXOTE *in half-light reverentially affixing the token
to his helmet; and in half-light also,* ALDONZA *in the
kitchen studying with mixed emotions the missive which
she cannot read*)

> To each his Dulcinea,
> That he alone can name . . .
> To each a secret hiding place
> Where he can find the haunting face
> To light his secret flame.

> For with his Dulcinea
> Beside him so to stand,
> A man can do quite anything,
> Outfly the bird upon the wing,
> Hold moonlight in his hand.

> Yet if you build your life on dreams
> It's prudent to recall,
> A man with moonlight in his hand
> Has nothing there at all.

> There is no Dulcinea,
> She's made of flame and air,
> And yet how lovely life would seem
> If every man could weave a dream
> To keep him from despair.

> To each his Dulcinea
> Though she's naught but flame and air!

>> (*The lights on the* PADRE *dim out, and he exits.
>> Music resumes in another motif as the lighting in
>> the courtyard—moonlight—comes to full.*
>>
>> QUIXOTE *is now pacing back and forth, lance in
>> hand, holding vigil over his armor*)

46

DON QUIXOTE (*Pausing*) Now must I consider how sages of the future will describe this historic night. (*He strikes a pose*) "Long after the sun had retired to his couch, darkening the gates and balconies of La Mancha, Don Quixote with measured tread and lofty expression held vigil in the courtyard of a mighty castle!" (*He hears the pompous echo of his voice, bows his head, ashamed*) Oh, maker of empty boasts. On this, of all nights, to give way to vanity. Nay, Don Quixote—take a deep breath of life and consider how it should be lived. (*He kneels*)
Call nothing thy own except thy soul.
Love not what thou art, but only what
    thou may become.
Do not pursue pleasure, for thou may have
    the misfortune to overtake it.
Look always forward; in last year's nest
    there are no birds this year.
    (ALDONZA *has entered the courtyard en route to her rendezvous with* PEDRO. *She stops, watching* DON QUIXOTE *and listening*)
Be just to all men. Be courteous to all women.
Live in the vision of that one for whom great deeds
    are done . . . she that is called Dulcinea.

ALDONZA Why do you call me that?

DON QUIXOTE (*He opens his eyes*) My lady!

ALDONZA Oh, get up from there. Get up! (DON QUIXOTE *rises worshipfully*) Why do you call me by that name?

DON QUIXOTE Because it is thine.

ALDONZA My name is Aldonza!

DON QUIXOTE (*Shakes his head respectfully*) I know thee, lady.

ALDONZA   My name is Aldonza and I think you know me *not.*

DON QUIXOTE   All my years I have known thee. Thy virtue. Thy nobility of spirit.

ALDONZA   (*Laughs scornfully, whips the rebozo from her head*)   Take another look!

DON QUIXOTE   (*Gently*)   I have already seen thee in my heart.

ALDONZA   Your heart doesn't know much about women!

DON QUIXOTE   It knows all, my lady. They are the soul of man . . . the radiance that lights his way. A woman is . . . glory!

ALDONZA   (*Anger masking uncertainty*)   What do you want of me?

DON QUIXOTE   Nothing.

ALDONZA   Liar!

DON QUIXOTE   (*Bows his head*)   I deserved the rebuke. I ask of my lady—

ALDONZA   *Now* we get to it.

DON QUIXOTE   . . . that I may be allowed to serve her. That I may hold her in my heart. That I may dedicate each victory and call upon her in defeat. And if at last I give my life I give it in the sacred name of Dulcinea.

ALDONZA   (*Draws her rebozo about her shoulders and backs away, shaken*)   I must go . . . Pedro is waiting . . . (*She pauses. Vehemently*) Why do you do these things?

DON QUIXOTE   What things, my lady?

ALDONZA   These ridiculous . . . the things you do!

DON QUIXOTE   I hope to add some measure of grace to the world.

ALDONZA   The world's a dungheap and we are maggots that crawl on it!

DON QUIXOTE   My lady knows better in her heart.

ALDONZA   What's in *my* heart will get me halfway to hell. And you, Señor Don Quixote—you're going to take such a beating!

DON QUIXOTE   Whether I win or lose does not matter.

ALDONZA   What does?

DON QUIXOTE   Only that I follow the quest.

ALDONZA   (*Spits in vulgar contempt*) *That* for your quest. (*She turns, marches away, then stops. Music: very softly, as she comes back*) What does it mean— quest?

DON QUIXOTE   The mission of each true knight . . . his duty—nay, his privilege! (*He sings*)
To dream the impossible dream,
To fight the unbeatable foe,
To bear with unbearable sorrow,
To run where the brave dare not go.

To right the unrightable wrong,
To love, pure and chaste, from afar,
To try, when your arms are too weary,
To reach the unreachable star!

This is my Quest, to follow that star,
No matter how hopeless, no matter how far,
To fight for the right without question or pause,
To be willing to march into hell for a heavenly cause!

And I know, if I'll only be true to this glorious quest,
That my heart will lie peaceful and calm when I'm
    laid to my rest.

And the world will be better for this,
That one man, scorned and covered with scars,
Still strove, with his last ounce of courage,
To reach the unreachable stars!

ALDONZA (*Is quite still after the song. Then pleading suddenly*) Once—just once—would you look at me as I really am?

DON QUIXOTE (*Lowering his eyes to gaze into hers*) I see beauty. Purity. I see the woman each man holds secret within him. Dulcinea.
> (ALDONZA *moans in inexpressible despair. She backs away from the steady eyes, shaking her head. She turns to run—and gasps as she collides with* PEDRO, *who has approached unseen. He grips her in fury*)

PEDRO Keep me waiting, will you?

ALDONZA I wasn't—I didn't—

PEDRO (*Mocking ferociously*) My lady. My princess!
> (*And he slaps her so that she goes spinning to the ground*)

DON QUIXOTE (*A roar of outrage*) Monster!

PEDRO Stay clear!

DON QUIXOTE (*Advancing*) Thou wouldst strike a woman?!

PEDRO Stand back or I'll break your empty head!

DON QUIXOTE Oh, thou heart of flint and bowels of cork! Now shall I chastise thee!

PEDRO   I warn you—ai-e-ee! (DON QUIXOTE, *clubbing his lance, catches* PEDRO *alongside the head, sending him sprawling. Music begins under.* PEDRO *groans*) Oh-h-h, I am killed. (*In a yell, staying on the ground*) Jose! Tenorio! Muleteers!

> (*The* MULETEERS *approach on the run.* ALDONZA *is back on her feet, and has sheltered herself behind the watering-trough.* SANCHO *comes running from the inn*)

DON QUIXOTE   (*Facing the reinforcements*)   Come one, come all! Don Quixote will vanquish armies!

PEDRO   Beware the lance!

ALDONZA   (*Stepping out*)   Let him be!

PEDRO   Back, whore!

ALDONZA   I said let him be! He's worth a thousand of you!

PEDRO   (*Diverted from* DON QUIXOTE)   You want the same, eh?

> (*He lurches toward her.* ALDONZA *snatches* DON QUIXOTE's *sword from the watering-trough, swings it in a mighty arc, and the flat of the blade sends* PEDRO *bowling butt over elbow.*
>
> *Music comes up full, as* QUIXOTE *charges back into the fray. A comic-choreographic treatment of the conflict.* QUIXOTE *wields the lance.* ALDONZA *swings hugely with the flat of the sword, and* SANCHO *makes himself useful to both. The battle rages, and finally the* MULETEERS, *with cries, groans, and howls of pain, fall hors de combat. The music fades out*)

DON QUIXOTE (*Gasping but joyful*) Victory!

SANCHO Victory!

ALDONZA (*Brandishing the sword*) Victory!
(*The* INNKEEPER *roused from sleep, comes rushing on, wearing nightgown and bedcap*)

INNKEEPER What is this? All the noise—! (*He sees the* MULETEERS *where they lie groaning in an untidy heap and is aghast*) Oh! Oh! What dreadful thing . . . ?

ALDONZA What *glorious* thing!

DON QUIXOTE (*Gasping*) Sir Castellano—I would inform you—that the right has triumphed.
(*He sags to the ground*)

SANCHO (*Hurrying to him*) Your Grace! Are you hurt?

DON QUIXOTE Nay . . . a little weakness . . .

ALDONZA Oh, he *is* hurt!
(*She drops the sword and hurries to help.* MARIA, *frightened and in nightclothes, comes running out*)

MARIA What is it? (*Sees* QUIXOTE) The madman! I knew it!

INNKEEPER Fetch bandages! Hurry!

ALDONZA (*Tearing bandages from her petticoat*) Poor warrior . . .

MARIA (*Bitterly*) Poor lunatic!

INNKEEPER Go back to bed, Maria.

MARIA I warned you what would happen!

INNKEEPER *Go to bed.*
> (MARIA *exits haughtily, as the* INNKEEPER *hauls one of the* MULETEERS *out of the well.* DON QUIXOTE *stirs and moans*)

SANCHO He's coming around!

DON QUIXOTE (*Opens his eyes and is looking at* ALDONZA, *weakly but with pleasure*) Ah . . . might I always wake to such a vision!

ALDONZA Don't move.

SANCHO I must say, Your Grace, we certainly did a job out here.

DON QUIXOTE We routed them, did we?

ALDONZA Ha! *That* bunch'll be walking bowlegged for a week!

DON QUIXOTE (*Distressed*) My lady! It is not seemly to gloat over the fallen.

ALDONZA Let 'em rot in hell!
> (*By now the last of the* MULETEERS *have been helped from the courtyard*)

INNKEEPER (*Agitated, to* DON QUIXOTE) Sir, I am a tame and peaceful man. Please, Sir Knight—I don't like to be inhospitable—but I must ask you to leave as soon as you are able.

DON QUIXOTE (*With dignity*) I am sorry to have offended the dignity of thy castle and I shall depart with daylight. But first, my lord, I must remind thee of thy promise.

INNKEEPER Promise?

DON QUIXOTE   True, it is not yet dawn, but I have kept vigil and proven myself in combat. Therefore I beg thou dub me knight.

INNKEEPER *(Remembering)*   Oh-h. Certainly. Let's get it over with.

DON QUIXOTE *(To* SANCHO*)*   Wilt be good enough to fetch my sword? *(Warmly, as* ALDONZA *assists)* Lady, I cannot tell thee how joyful I am that this ceremony should take place in thy presence.

ALDONZA *(As he sways)*   Be careful, now!

DON QUIXOTE   It is a solemn moment which seals my vocation . . .

> *(*SANCHO *hands* QUIXOTE'S *sword to the* INN-KEEPER*)*

INNKEEPER *(Handling the sword gingerly)*   Are you ready?

DON QUIXOTE   I am.

INNKEEPER   Very well, then. Kneel! *(Music begins as* DON QUIXOTE, *with* ALDONZA *and* SANCHO *assisting on either side, gets down to his knees. He intones)*
Don Quixote de La Mancha!
I hereby dub thee knight.
> *(He touches him with the sword on each shoulder, then hands the sword back to* SANCHO *and starts to exit)*

DON QUIXOTE *(As music continues)*   Your Lordship.

INNKEEPER   Didn't I do it right?

DON QUIXOTE *(Humbly)*   If Your Lordship would make some mention of the deeds I performed to earn this honor . . . ?

INNKEEPER Oh . . . of course. (*He gets the sword back from* SANCHO. *He intones*)
> Don Quixote de La Mancha,
> Having proven yourself this day
> In glorious and terrible combat
> And by my authority as lord of this castle—
> I hereby dub thee knight!
>> (*He gives the sword back to* SANCHO, *again starts to leave*)

DON QUIXOTE Your Lordship . . .

INNKEEPER (*Stopping again*) Something else?
> (*This time* SANCHO *hands the sword back to him*)

DON QUIXOTE It is customary to grant the new knight an added name. If Your Lordship could devise such a name for me . . . ?

INNKEEPER Hmmm. (*He reflects a moment, looking at the battered face. He gets an inspiration and sings*)
> Hail, Knight of the Woeful Countenance,
> Knight of the Woeful Countenance!
> Wherever you go
> People will know
> Of the glorious deeds of the Knight of the Woe—
> Ful Countenance!
>
> Farewell and good cheer, oh my brave cavalier,
> Ride onward to glorious strife.
> I swear when you're gone I'll remember you well
> For all of the rest of my life!
>
> Hail, Knight of the Woeful Countenance,
> Knight of the Woeful Countenance!
> Wherever you go,
> Face to the foe,

55

They will quail at the sight of the Knight of the
     Woe—
Ful Countenance!

Oh valorous knight, go and fight for the right,
And battle all villains that be.
But oh, when you do, what will happen to you
Thank God I won't be there to see!

INNKEEPER, ALDONZA and SANCHO
     Hail, Knight of the Woeful Countenance!
     Knight of the Woeful Countenance!
     Wherever you go
     People will know
     Of the glorious deeds of the Knight of the Woe—
     Ful count—te—nance!

DON QUIXOTE (*Ecstatically*)   I thank thee.

INNKEEPER (*Handing the sword to* QUIXOTE)   Now, Sir
Knight, I am going to bed. And I advise you to do the
same!
     (*He exits*)

DON QUIXOTE (*Still on his knees; raptly*)   Knight of the
Woeful Countenance . . .

ALDONZA (*In tears*)   It's a *beautiful* name.

SANCHO   Come, Your Grace. (*Helping him to his feet*)
Let's get you to bed.

DON QUIXOTE   Not yet. I owe something to my enemies.

ALDONZA   *That* account's been paid!

DON QUIXOTE   No, my lady. I must raise them up and minister to their wounds.

ALDONZA (*Aghast*)   What?

56

DON QUIXOTE   Nobility demands.

ALDONZA   It does?

DON QUIXOTE   Yes, my lady. Therefore I shall take these—

ALDONZA (*Firmly, snatching up the bandages*)   No, you won't. *I'll* take them. *I'll* minister.

DON QUIXOTE   But—

ALDONZA (*Simply*)   They were my enemies, too.

DON QUIXOTE (*With emotion*)   Oh, blessed one . . . !

SANCHO (*Helping* QUIXOTE)   Come, Your Grace.

DON QUIXOTE (*As they exit*)   Blessed one! Ah, blessed one . . . !

> (*The lighting changes as* ALDONZA *enters the interior of the Inn. The* MULETEERS *lie about the room, moaning, licking their wounds.* PEDRO *lifts his head as he sees her*)

PEDRO (*In a growl*)   What do you think you're doing?

ALDONZA (*Matter-of-factly*)   I'm going to minister to your wounds.

PEDRO   You're . . . *what?*

ALDONZA   Nobility demands. (*Kneeling beside* JOSE) Turn over, you poxy goat.

> (JOSE's *eyes light up with cat-and-mouse savagery as* ALDONZA *bends over him. With a shout he seizes her, and the other* MULETEERS *pounce upon her, also.*
>
> *Music: a sardonic version of "Little Bird" as with methodical, ritualistic brutality, in choreographic staging the* MULETEERS *bind, gag, beat and ravage*

ALDONZA. *She fights back as best she can but the fight is hopeless and she must submit.* FERMINA *enters and watches, sadistically gleeful over the humiliation of* ALDONZA.

Finally PEDRO, *realizing that* ALDONZA *is unconscious, signals the others to stop.* JOSE *slings the brutalized* ALDONZA *over his back and the* MULE-TEERS *exit, carrying her off. As they do so, the lights pick up* QUIXOTE *and* SANCHO *at another area of the stage*)

DON QUIXOTE (*Raptly*) Ah, Sancho, how I do envy my enemies.

SANCHO *Envy?*

DON QUIXOTE To think they know the healing touch of my lady Dulcinea! (*An ecstatic sigh*) Let this be proof to thee, Sancho. Nobility triumphs. Virtue always prevails. (*Uplifted*) Now in the moment of victory do I confirm my knighthood and my oath. For all my life, this I do swear—(*Singing*)
To dream the impossible dream,
To fight the unbeatable foe,
To bear with unbearable sorrow,
To run where the brave dare not go!
(*Off, faintly at first, then growing, is heard the "Inquisition Theme."* QUIXOTE *falters and falls silent.* CERVANTES, *losing the character of* QUIXOTE, *comes forward as the volume of the theme grows and the setting alters back to the prison. The* PRISONERS *are immobile, cocking their heads to listen*)

CERVANTES (*Uncertainly*) That sound . . . ?

THE GOVERNOR   The Men of the Inquisition.

CERVANTES   What does it mean?

PRISONER   They're coming to fetch someone.

PRISONER   They'll haul him off—put the question to him.

PRISONER   Next thing he knows—he's burning!

CERVANTES   Are they coming for me?

THE DUKE   Very possibly. What, Cervantes? Not *afraid?*
(CERVANTES *shakes his head dumbly. Mockingly*)
Where's your courage? Is that in your imagination, too?
(CERVANTES *is retreating,* THE DUKE *following inexorably*) No escape, Cervantes. This is *happening.* Not
to your brave man of La Mancha, but to *you.* Quick,
Cervantes—call upon him. Let him shield you. Let him
save you, if he can, from *that!*
  (*On the stairway the* MEN OF THE INQUISITION *appear. They are robed, hooded, frightening in aspect.*
CERVANTES *is paralyzed with fear, only his eyes
moving, following them as they descend into the
vault. As they approach* CERVANTES, *the* GUARDS
*open the floor-trap and drag up a prisoner. They
haul him up the stairs.* CERVANTES *sinks to a bench,
faintly.*
  *The "Inquisition Theme" recedes, fading as the
stairway is withdrawn.* THE GOVERNOR *snaps his fingers at a* PRISONER, *who brings a goatskin of wine,
hands it to* CERVANTES, *who takes it with trembling
hands and drinks deeply*)

THE GOVERNOR   Better?

CERVANTES (*Faintly*)   Thank you . . .

THE GOVERNOR Good, let's get on with your defense!

CERVANTES If I might rest a moment . . .

THE DUKE (*With tolerant contempt*) This La Mancha
—what is it like?

THE GOVERNOR An empty place. Great wide plains.

PRISONER A desert.

THE GOVERNOR A wasteland.

THE DUKE Which apparently grows lunatics.

CERVANTES I would say, rather . . . men of illusion.

THE DUKE Much the same. Why are you poets so fasci-
nated with madmen?

CERVANTES I suppose . . . we have much in common.

THE DUKE You both turn your backs on life.

CERVANTES We both select from life what pleases us.

THE DUKE A man must come to terms with life as it is!

CERVANTES I have lived nearly fifty years, and I have seen
life as it is. Pain, misery, hunger . . . cruelty beyond
belief. I have heard the singing from taverns and the
moans from bundles of filth on the streets. I have been
a soldier and seen my comrades fall in battle . . . or die
more slowly under the lash in Africa. I have held them
in my arms at the final moment. These were men who
saw life as it is, yet they died despairing. No glory, no
gallant last words . . . only their eyes filled with con-
fusion, whimpering the question: "Why?" I do not think
they asked why they were dying, but why they had lived.
(*He rises, and through the following speech moves into*

the character of DON QUIXOTE *as a musical underscore and change of setting begin)* When life itself seems lunatic, who knows where madness lies? Perhaps to be too practical is madness. To surrender dreams—this may be madness. To seek treasure where there is only trash. Too much sanity may be madness. And maddest of all, to see life as it is and not as it should be.

> *(The music has stated the "I Am I, Don Quixote" theme thinly during the preceding speech, and the prison and* PRISONERS *have disappeared.* CERVANTES *is isolated in limbo; the "horses" have appeared. The lights change)*

DON QUIXOTE *(Singing)*

> I am I, Don Quixote,
> The Lord of La Mancha,
> Destroyer of evil am I,
> I will march to the sound of the trumpets of glory,
> Forever to conquer or die!

SANCHO   I don't understand.

DON QUIXOTE   What, my friend?

SANCHO   Why you're so cheerful. First you find your lady, then you lose her.

DON QUIXOTE   Never lost!

SANCHO   Well, she ran off with those mule drivers . . . ?

DON QUIXOTE   Ah, but undoubtedly with some high purpose.

SANCHO   High purpose with those low characters?

DON QUIXOTE   Sancho, Sancho, always thine eye sees evil in preference to good.

SANCHO (*Stubbornly*) There's no use blaming my eye; it doesn't make the world, it only sees it. (*A band of* MOORS *appears*) Anyway, there's something my eye sees truly enough. Moors! Let's make a wide track around them, for they're a scurvy lot and Your Grace can't deny *that*.

DON QUIXOTE There, thou fallest into the trap of thy peasant mind again.

SANCHO They're *not* thieves and murderers?

DON QUIXOTE Do not condemn before thou knowest! (*The* MOORISH GIRL *undulates toward them*) Sh-h-h—a young innocent approaches. (*The girl dances lasciviously as her* PIMP *encourages her, whining a nasal obbligato*) Charming!

SANCHO (*In protest*) But she's a trollop, and he—why he's nothing but a—!

DON QUIXOTE Have done with these foul suspicions! Dost not understand what they are saying? These two are brother and sister, offspring of the noble African lord, Sidi ben Mali. (*The girl approaches* QUIXOTE) Sweet maiden, what wilt thou?

SANCHO I think *I* know what she wilt!
    (*The* GIRL *seizes one of* QUIXOTE's *hands and presses it to her right breast*)

DON QUIXOTE She wishes me to feel the beating of her heart. And such is her innocence she does not even know where it is.
    (*The* GIRL *seizes* QUIXOTE's *other hand and presses it to her other breast*)

SANCHO (*Cynically*) Or even how many she has!
    (*The* MOORS *dance and wail; the* PIMP *caterwauls, beating his breast*)

The KNIGHT OF THE MIRRORS, played by Jon Cypher, confronts and confuses DON QUIXOTE, played by Richard Kiley, with shields that reflect images of himself.

DON QUIXOTE (*Listening gravely*) Much as I surmised.

SANCHO What's he saying?

DON QUIXOTE A most grievous tale. The noble Sidi ben Mali hath been taken captive and even now lies deep in a dungeon not five leagues from here. While these, his faithful family and retainers, travel the countryside in hope of raising a ransom. (*The* GIRL *dances, putting a coin on her forehead*) See, Sancho, how quaint the customs of these Africans! In this charming manner they ask that I make contribution to their cause.

SANCHO Don't do it!

DON QUIXOTE (*Incredulously*) Thou would'st ignore a fellow knight in jeopardy? Here, sweet maiden—with all my heart. (*He gives money to the* GIRL, *and the other* MOORS *take the opportunity to lift his money pouch and other belongings. Meanwhile, to* SANCHO) Shame on thee for a reluctant Christian! Shame on thee for a parsimonious wretch! Shame on thee for a small-hearted peasant! Shame on thee, Sancho, multiple shame! (SANCHO, *overcome by the rebuke, drops a coin in* QUI-XOTE's *golden helmet which the* GIRL *is holding*) Ah, Sancho, I knew it, I knew thy heart was good! (*The* MOORS *dance wildly*) How inspiring is their gratitude. Let us celebrate in their fashion!

> (QUIXOTE *and* SANCHO *join the dance; the* MOORS *steal everything in sight, including the "horses."* QUIXOTE *and* SANCHO *finally fall, exhausted but happy. Then, as they discover with dismay what has befallen them, the lights black out.*
>
> *The lights come up on the courtyard of the Inn. The* INNKEEPER, *humming happily, is crossing the courtyard. From offstage, the discordant bleat of*

SANCHO's *bugle. He stops and turns a haunted face toward the gates.* MARIA *comes crashing from the inn*)

MARIA (*A shriek*) Don't open the gates! Don't let him in!

INNKEEPER (*His face clearing*) It's the pig-butcher. Don't you remember? We expected him yesterday.

MARIA No, no! Don't open!
(*The* INNKEEPER *goes to the gates as* QUIXOTE *and* SANCHO *appear, supporting each other.* MARIA *screams and runs off*)

INNKEEPER Not *again?* (*Trying to bar the way*) This place is closed. This castle has gone out of business!

DON QUIXOTE (*Feeble but stern*) What, sir? Deny the right of sanctuary?

INNKEEPER I hate to, but—

DON QUIXOTE *And* to a knight dubbed by thy own hand?

INNKEEPER (*Wavering*) It *doesn't* seem right . . .

DON QUIXOTE Not by any rule of chivalry!
(*The* INNKEEPER, *yielding with a sigh, allows them to enter.* QUIXOTE *and* SANCHO *totter into the court-yard—footsore and in very bad shape. The* INNKEEPER *looks them over*)

INNKEEPER More muleteers?

SANCHO (*Hollowly*) Moors. They stole our money.

DON QUIXOTE Have done, Sancho.

SANCHO They stole our animals.

DON QUIXOTE   Must thou harp on it?

SANCHO   They stole everything we *had*.

INNKEEPER (*With pity*)   Why don't you declare a truce?

DON QUIXOTE   And allow wickedness to flourish?

INNKEEPER   I'm afraid wickedness wears thick armor.
(*In the background, unseen by the three,* ALDONZA *enters*)

DON QUIXOTE (*Roused*)   And for that wouldst thou have me surrender? Nay, let a man be overthrown ten thousand times, still must he rise and again do battle. The Enchanter may confuse the outcome, but the effort remains sublime!

ALDONZA (*Bitterly*)   Lies. Madness and lies.

INNKEEPER (*Horrified at her bruises, her tattered rags*) Aldonza! What happened?

ALDONZA   Ask *him*.

INNKEEPER (*Calling as he exits*)   Maria! Maria!

DON QUIXOTE (*Rising, aghast*)   I shall punish them that did this crime.

ALDONZA   Crime! You know the worst crime of all? Being born. For that you get punished your whole life!

DON QUIXOTE   Dulcinea—

ALDONZA   Enough of that! Get yourself to a madhouse. Rave about nobility where no one can hear!

DON QUIXOTE   My lady—

ALDONZA (*Passionately*)   I am not your lady! I am not any kind of a lady! (*Singing*)

I was spawned in a ditch by a mother who left me
    there
Naked and cold and too hungry to cry;
I never blamed her, I'm sure she left hoping
That I'd have the good sense to die!

Then, of course, there's my father—I'm told that
    young ladies
Can point to their fathers with maidenly pride;
Mine was some regiment here for an hour,
I can't even tell you which side!

So of course I became, as befitted my delicate birth,
The most casual bride of the murdering scum of the
    earth!

DON QUIXOTE   And still thou art my lady.

ALDONZA   And still he torments me! Lady! How should I
be a lady? (*Singing*)
    For a lady has modest and maidenly airs
    And a virtue I somehow suspect that I lack;
    It's hard to remember those maidenly airs
    In a stable laid flat on your back.

    Won't you look at me, look at me, God, won't you
        look at me,
    Look at the kitchen slut reeking of sweat!
    Born on a dungheap to die on a dungheap,
    A strumpet men use and forget!

    If you feel that you see me not quite at my virginal
        best,
    Cross my palm with a coin and I'll willingly show you
        the rest!

DON QUIXOTE (*Tenderly*)   Never deny, thou art Dulcinea.

ALDONZA (*Ever more frantically*) Take the clouds from your eyes and see me as I really am! (*Singing*)
> You have shown me the sky, but what good is the sky
> To a creature who'll never do better than crawl?
> Of all the cruel bastards who've badgered and battered me,
> You are the cruelest of all!
>
> Can't you see what your gentle insanities do to me?
> Rob me of anger and give me despair!
> Blows and abuse I can take and give back again,
> Tenderness I cannot bear!
>
> So please torture me now with your "Sweet Dulcineas" no more!
> I am no one! I'm nothing! I'm only Aldonza the whore!

DON QUIXOTE Now and forever thou art my lady Dulcinea!

ALDONZA (*A wail*) No-o-o!
> (*She collapses, despairing.* DON QUIXOTE *moves toward her compassionately—but suddenly, off, there is a fanfare of trumpets. Brazen, warlike, ominous in quality.* SANCHO *scurries to look, then backs away from what he sees*)

SANCHO (*Choking with fear*) Master . . . !
> (*Music continues as the gates swing open. A strange cavalcade enters; liveried attendants preceding a* KNIGHT, *tall and terrifying in fantastic armor. He wears a chain-mail tunic on which are mounted tiny mirrors that glitter and dazzle the eye. On his head is a masklike casque, only his eyes visible through slits. From the crest of the casque spring great plumes, accentuating what*)

seems already incredible stature. In his hand is a naked, shining sword. The music cuts as the cavalcade comes to a halt)

KNIGHT OF THE MIRRORS *(His voice harsh, clangorous)* Is there one here calls himself Don Quixote de La Mancha? If there is—and he be not afraid to look upon me—let him stand forth!

DON QUIXOTE *(At length, voice shaking)* I am Don Quixote, Knight of the Woeful Countenance.

KNIGHT OF THE MIRRORS *(Voice magnified and metallic within the casque)* Now hear me, thou charlatan! Thou art no knight, but a foolish pretender. Thy pretense is a child's mockery, and thy principles dirt beneath my feet!

DON QUIXOTE *(Trembling with anger)* Oh, false knight! Discourteous! Before I chastise thee, tell me thy name.

KNIGHT OF THE MIRRORS Thou shalt hear it in due course.

DON QUIXOTE Then say why thou seekest me out!

KNIGHT OF THE MIRRORS *(Mockingly)* Thou called upon *me*, Don Quixote. Thou reviled me and threatened.

DON QUIXOTE The Enchanter! *(A moan from* SANCHO. *The music, under, is the "Enchanter's Theme."* DON QUIXOTE *tears off his left gauntlet, flinging it at the* KNIGHT's *feet)* Behold at thy feet the gage of battle!

SANCHO *(Anguished)* Master—no!
(He runs, scrambles for the gauntlet, but the KNIGHT *pins it with his sword)*

KNIGHT OF THE MIRRORS *(Suddenly very cold)* On what terms do we fight?

68

DON QUIXOTE   Choose thine own!

KNIGHT OF THE MIRRORS   Very well. If thou art beaten thy freedom is forfeit and thou must obey my every command. (DON QUIXOTE *bows coldly*) And thy conditions?

DON QUIXOTE   If thou art still alive thou shalt kneel and beg mercy of my lady Dulcinea.

KNIGHT OF THE MIRRORS (*Mockingly*)   Where shall I find this lady?

DON QUIXOTE   There she stands.
   (*The* KNIGHT OF THE MIRRORS *turns his eyes to* AL-DONZA—*her rags, her bruises, her ruined face. He begins to laugh in cruel derision*)

KNIGHT OF THE MIRRORS   Thy lady . . . is an alley cat!

DON QUIXOTE (*Drawing his sword in fury*)   Monster! Defend thyself!

KNIGHT OF THE MIRRORS (*Stepping back*)   Hold! Thou asked my name, Don Quixote. Now I shall tell it. I am called—the Knight of the Mirrors! (*Music: the "Enchanter's Theme," as the* KNIGHT *swings forward his shield. Its surface is polished steel, a mirror which blinds and bewilders* DON QUIXOTE. *The* ATTENDANTS *reveal similar mirrors. In a choreographic pattern* QUIXOTE *will reel from one to the other, fetching up always against his own image*) Look, Don Quixote! Look in the mirror of reality and behold things as they truly are. Look! What seest thou, Don Quixote? A gallant knight? Naught but an aging fool! (*DON QUIXOTE recoils from his own image, only to be brought up against another*) Look! Dost thou see him? A madman dressed for a masquerade! (*Attempting escape,* QUIXOTE *finds himself facing another mirror*) Look, Don Quixote! See him as he truly is! See the clown! (QUIXOTE *reels away, only to find the mirrors converging as the* KNIGHT *and his* ATTENDANTS *close down upon him*) Drown, Don Quixote. Drown—drown in the mirror. Go deep—the masquerade is ended! (QUIXOTE *collapses to his knees*) Confess! Thy lady is a trollop, and thy dream the nightmare of a disordered mind!

DON QUIXOTE (*In dazed desperation*) I am Don Quixote, knight-errant of La Mancha . . . and my lady is the Lady Dulcinea. I am Don Quixote, knight-errant . . . and my lady . . . my lady . . .
(*Beaten, weeping, he sinks to the floor*)

KNIGHT OF THE MIRRORS (*Removing the casque from his head*) It is done!

SANCHO (*Thunderstruck*) Your Grace! It is Doctor Carrasco! It is only Sansón Carrasco!

DR. CARRASCO Forgive me, Señor Quijana. It was the only way.
(*Lights dim down to* DON QUIXOTE, *huddled weeping on the floor.* ALDONZA *comes toward him, her face devastated by loss and pity. Music bridges as the lighting alters back to that of the prison, and the* CAPTAIN OF THE INQUISITION *is seen entering*)

CAPTAIN (*Shouting*) Cervantes! Cervantes! Prepare to be summoned!

CERVANTES (*Confusedly*) By whom?

CAPTAIN The Judges of the Inquisition!

THE GOVERNOR Captain! How soon?

CAPTAIN Soon!
   (*He exits*)

THE GOVERNOR But not yet. (*To* CERVANTES, *with satis-faction*) Good. You'll have time to finish the story.

CERVANTES But the story is finished.

THE GOVERNOR *What?*

CERVANTES At least so far as I know it.

THE GOVERNOR I don't think I like this ending. (*A growl from the* PRISONERS) I don't think the jury likes it, either.

THE DUKE Well, then—he's failed!

THE GOVERNOR Miguel de Cervantes. It is the sentence of this court—

CERVANTES (*Panicky*) Wait!

THE GOVERNOR For what?

CERVANTES If I could have a little more time?

THE GOVERNOR (*After a glance at the* PRISONERS) Oh, *I'll* grant it. But the Inquisition . . . ?

CERVANTES A few moments only! Let me improvise . . .
   (*He snaps his fingers, pointing out the* PRISONERS *who are to play in the following scene. Music underscores: a melancholy version of "I'm Only Thinking of Him" as the setting is improvised in the shape of a bedroom in* ALONSO QUIJANA's *home. Lighting alters to shafts of dying sun as the bed and its occupant—*DON QUIXOTE—*are revealed.*
   QUIXOTE's *eyes are open but deep-hollowed and remote, windows on a mind that has retreated to*

some secret place. There is silence a while but for the music)

ANTONIA *(Voice low, to* CARRASCO*)* Can you do *nothing?*

PADRE *(With soft compassion)* I'm afraid there'll be more need of my services than his. *(Waves a hand slowly across* QUIXOTE's *unseeing eyes)* Where is he, I wonder? In what dark cavern of the mind?

DR. CARRASCO According to recent theory—

PADRE Doctor. Please.

DR. CARRASCO *(Resentfully)* Don't you think I did right?

PADRE *(Sighing)* Yes. There's the contradiction . . .
    *(*SANCHO *enters timidly, hat in hand)*

ANTONIA You again?

DR. CARRASCO Tell him to go away.

PADRE *(Wearily)* What harm can he do?

ANTONIA Yes—it's all been done!
    (She lets him pass, grudgingly)

SANCHO *(Bobbing his head to the* PADRE*)* Your Reverence. *(Diffidently)* Could I talk to him?

PADRE I'm afraid he won't hear you.

SANCHO Well, then, I won't say much.

DR. CARRASCO And no mention of knight-errantry!

SANCHO Of course not. Does one speak of the rope in the house of the hanged? Oh—excuse me, Your Grace.

ANTONIA *(Bitterly)* Your Grace.

72

SANCHO (*Seating himself by the bed*) Just a few words
. . . to lighten his heart. (*Music: he sings*)
> A little gossip . . . a little chat . . .
> A little idle talk . . . of this and that . . .
> I'll tell him all the troubles I have had
> And since he doesn't hear, at least he won't feel bad.
> (*To* QUIXOTE)
> When I first got home my wife Teresa beat me,
> But the blows fell very lightly on my back.
> She kept missing every other stroke and crying from
>   the heart
> That while I was gone she'd gone and lost the knack!
> (*Spoken*)

Of course I hit her back, Your Grace, but she's a lot
harder than I am, and you know what they say—
"Whether the stone hits the pitcher or the pitcher hits
the stone, it's going to be bad for the pitcher." So I've
got bruises from here to—
> (*An admonishing look from the* PADRE. *He sings*)
> A little gossip . . . a little chat . . .
> A little idle talk . . . of this and that . . .
> If no one listens, then it's just as well,
> At least I won't get caught in any lies I tell!
> (*Conspiratorially to* QUIXOTE)
> Oh, I haven't fought a windmill in a fortnight,
> And the humble joys get duller every day.
> Why, when I'm asleep a dragon with his fiery
>   tongue a-waggin'
> Whispers, "Sancho, won't you please come out and
>   play?"

DR. CARRASCO (*Roused*) That's enough now.

SANCHO Why? What did I do?

DR. CARRASCO I warned you!

SANCHO I didn't do anything, I was only trying to—

DON QUIXOTE (*Barely audible*) My friend.

SANCHO (*Politely, as all turn, startled*) Did Your Grace say something?

DON QUIXOTE You're a fat little bag stuffed with proverbs.

SANCHO Yes, Your Grace. Well, as I was saying—

ANTONIA (*Running to* QUIXOTE) Uncle!

DON QUIXOTE My dear . . . (*His eyes go to the others*) Good morning, Padre . . . or is it evening?

PADRE Alonso . . .

DR. CARRASCO How do you feel, sir?

DON QUIXOTE Not well, my friends.

DR. CARRASCO Can you speak your name?

DON QUIXOTE (*Puzzled*) Should a man not know his own name?

DR. CARRASCO If you would say it . . . ?

DON QUIXOTE (*In surprise*) Alonso Quijana. (DR. CARRASCO *gives a triumphant look to the others*) Padre . . .

PADRE Here beside you.

DON QUIXOTE I should like to make a will.

PADRE Of course.
      (*He exits to get materials*)

ANTONIA (*Anxiously, as* DON QUIXOTE *closes his eyes and is silent*) Uncle . . . ?

74

DON QUIXOTE (*Faintly*) Forgive me, my dear. When I close my eyes I see a pale horse . . . and he beckons me—mount.

ANTONIA No, Uncle. You will get well!

DON QUIXOTE (*Smiling*) Why should a man get well when he is dying? It's such a waste of good health. (*With a feeble gesture*) Come closer, my friends. (*They come to the bedside*) In my illness I dreamed so strangely . . . Oh, such dreams! It seemed I was a . . . no . . . I dare not tell lest you think me mad.

ANTONIA Put them from your mind!

DON QUIXOTE (*Deeply weary*) They are gone, my dear . . . nor do I know what they meant. (*As the* PADRE *re-enters*) Padre . . . ?

PADRE Speak, my friend, and I shall write.

DON QUIXOTE I, Alonso Quijana . . . with one foot in the stirrup and the agony of death already upon me . . .
(*The* PADRE's *pen scratches busily. From the front of the house the thudding of the doorknocker is heard*)

ANTONIA (*To the* HOUSEKEEPER *as she goes to see*) Don't admit *anyone*.

DON QUIXOTE . . . do hereby make the following disposition of my estate. The bulk I bequeath to my beloved niece, Antonia Quijana . . . (*From off comes a racket of voices in vehement argument*)—with the exception of certain personal bequests which are as follows—
(*The* HOUSEKEEPER *backs in, pushed roughly by* ALDONZA. *Everyone speaks at once*)

HOUSEKEEPER (*In fear and frenzy*) You cannot! I say you cannot!

ANTONIA What is this? Sansón!

ALDONZA Get out of my way, you hag—

DR. CARRASCO It's that slut from the Inn.

HOUSEKEEPER I tried to stop her! She threatened to—

ALDONZA Tear your eyes out!

DR. CARRASCO (*Advancing on* ALDONZA *grimly*) Get out of here.

ALDONZA And if you touch me again, by God—

DR. CARRASCO Get out of here!

ALDONZA Not before I see him!

DR. CARRASCO I'm warning you—go quietly or I'll—

DON QUIXOTE (*Voice weak but commanding*) Let be.

DR. CARRASCO Señor Quijana—

DON QUIXOTE In my house there will be courtesy! (DR. CARRASCO *reluctantly steps aside*) Come closer, girl. (ALDONZA *approaches*) Now. What is it you wish?

ALDONZA (*Incredulously*) Don't you know me?

DON QUIXOTE (*Puzzled*) Should I?

ALDONZA I am Aldonza!
(*A movement forward from the others. A pause*)

DON QUIXOTE (*Blankly*) I am sorry. I do not recall anyone of that name.

ALDONZA (*Looks about wildly. Sees* SANCHO. *Points to him*) He knows! (DON QUIXOTE's *eyes go to* SANCHO, *who steps forward as though to speak.* DR. CARRASCO

76

warns him fiercely with a gesture. SANCHO *closes his mouth, shrugs feebly. Panicky, to* DON QUIXOTE)
Please, my lord!

DON QUIXOTE (*Curiously*) Why do you say "my lord"? I am not a lord.

ALDONZA You are my lord, Don Quixote!
(*The others react, then hold very still*)

DON QUIXOTE Don Quixote. (*Rubs his forehead, troubled*) You must forgive me. I have been ill . . . I am confused by shadows. It is possible I knew you once, but I do not remember.
(ALDONZA *is stunned.* DR. CARRASCO *smoothly steps forward and takes her by the arm*)

DR. CARRASCO (*Moving her along*) This way.
(ALDONZA *allows herself to be led. But she stops, pulls loose suddenly, and in a rush comes back and flings herself to her knees beside the bed*)

ALDONZA Please! Try to remember!

DON QUIXOTE (*With helpless compassion*) Is it so important?

ALDONZA (*Anguished*) Everything. My whole life. You spoke to me and everything was—different!

DON QUIXOTE I . . . spoke to you?

ALDONZA And you looked at me! And you called me by another name! (*She sings, pleadingly*)
Dulcinea . . . Dulcinea . . .
Once you found a girl and called her Dulcinea,
When you spoke the name an angel seemed to whisper—
Dulcinea . . . Dulcinea . . .

77

(DR. CARRASCO *takes her by the arm, leads her toward the door but she resists, holding back to sing*)
Dulcinea . . . Dulcinea . . .
Won't you please bring back the dream of Dulcinea . . .
Won't you bring me back the bright and shining glory
Of Dulcinea . . . Dulcinea . . .

DR. CARRASCO   I'm afraid I must insist—

DON QUIXOTE   Let be! (*Disturbed, mind stirring*) Then perhaps . . . it was not a dream . . .

ALDONZA   You spoke of a dream. And about the Quest!

DON QUIXOTE   Quest?

ALDONZA   How you must fight and it doesn't matter whether you win or lose if only you follow the Quest!

DON QUIXOTE   The words. Tell me the words!

ALDONZA (*Speaking to music*)
   "To dream the impossible dream . . ."
But they're your own words!
   "To fight the unbeatable foe . . ."
Don't you remember?
   "To bear with unbearable sorrow . . ."
You must remember!
   "To run where the brave dare not go—"

DON QUIXOTE (*Remembering, speaks, then sings*)
   To right the unrightable wrong,

ALDONZA (*A whisper*)   Yes . . .

DON QUIXOTE
   To love, pure and chaste, from afar,

78

ALDONZA Yes . . .

DON QUIXOTE
    To try, when your arms are too weary,
    To reach the unreachable star!

ALDONZA (*Seizing his hand, kisses it*) Thank you, my lord!

DON QUIXOTE But this is not seemly, my lady. On thy knees? To me?

ALDONZA (*In protest as he tries to rise*) My lord, you are not well!

DON QUIXOTE (*Growing in power*) Not well? What is sickness to the body of a knight-errant? What matter wounds? For each time he falls he shall rise again—and woe to the wicked! (*A lusty bellow*) Sancho!

SANCHO Here, Your Grace!

DON QUIXOTE My armor! My sword!

SANCHO (*Delightedly, clapping his hands*) More misadventures!

DON QUIXOTE Adventures, old friend! (*Rising from the bed, and as* ALDONZA *and* SANCHO *support him on either side, he sings*)
    Oh the trumpets of glory now call me to ride,
    Yes, the trumpets are calling to me,
    And wherever I ride, ever staunch at my side,
    My squire and my lady shall be . . .

    I am I, Don Quixote—

DON QUIXOTE, ALDONZA and SANCHO
> The Lord of La Mancha,
> Our destiny calls and we go!
> And the wild winds of fortune shall carry us onward
> Oh, whithersoever . . .
>> (DON QUIXOTE *falters*)

ALDONZA (*A cry of apprehension*) My lord—!

SANCHO Master—!

DON QUIXOTE (*Reassuring them, sings on*)
> Whithersoever they blow,
> Onward to glory—
>> (*A sudden cry. A whisper*)
> . . . I . . . go . . .
>> (*He crumples to the floor*)

ANTONIA Uncle!
> (DR. CARRASCO *pushes* ALDONZA *aside and kneels to*
> DON QUIXOTE's *left. He bends over and places his*
> *ear to* QUIXOTE's *heart, then rises and goes to* AN-
> TONIA, *who is weeping softly. The* PADRE *comes to*
> QUIXOTE *and kneels. He crosses himself and chants*
> *in Latin*)

PADRE
> De profundis clamo ad te
> Domine, Domine,
>> (ALDONZA *goes slowly to* SANCHO)
> Audi vocem meam
> Fiant aures tuae intentae
> Ad vacem obse creationis meae
> Si delictarum
> Memoriam
> Serva neris . . .

SANCHO (*Stunned, pathetically*) He is dead. My master
is dead.

ALDONZA (*Quietly*)   A man died. He seemed a good man, but I did not know him.

SANCHO   But—

ALDONZA   Don Quixote is not dead. Believe, Sancho. Believe.

SANCHO (*In confused hope*)   Aldonza . . . ?

ALDONZA (*Gently*)   My name is Dulcinea.
(*The* PADRE's *hymn concludes as the lights dim out. In the darkness comes the snarling roll of the drums of the Inquisition; it gives way to chanting as lights fade in on the prison. The* CAPTAIN *enters at the head of the* MEN OF THE INQUISITION. *They descend to the vault.* CERVANTES, *kneeling, is removing the* DON QUIXOTE *beard and makeup*)

CAPTAIN (*Unrolling a scroll*)   Under authority of the Holy Office of the Inquisition! (*Reading*) "By reason of certain offenses committed against His Majesty's Most Catholic Church, the following is summoned to give answer and submit his person for purification if it be so ordered: Don Miguel de Cervantes."

CERVANTES (*With wry bravado*)   How popular a defendant I am. Summoned by one court before I've quite finished with another. Well? How says the Judge?

THE GOVERNOR (*Musingly, weighing the package now held in his hands*)   I think I know what this contains. The history of your mad knight? (CERVANTES *nods assent. Handing him the package*) Plead as well there as you did here and you may not burn.

CERVANTES   I've no intention of burning. (*To his* MAN-SERVANT, *buoyantly*) Well, old friend? Shall we go? (*He sees that the* SERVANT *is rigid with fear; comes to*

put a reassuring arm about his shoulder) Courage!
(He leads him toward the stairs)

THE GOVERNOR Cervantes. (CERVANTES *pauses*) I think
Don Quixote is brother to Don Miguel.

CERVANTES *(Smiling)* God help us—we are both men of
La Mancha.

> *(The* CAPTAIN *and the* HOODED MEN *about-face as
> the "Inquisition Theme" resumes. The cortège
> forms toward an exit, starts ascending the stairs.*
>
> *The* PRISONER *playing* ALDONZA *is standing apart
> from the other prisoners as she always does)*

PRISONER (ALDONZA) *(Singing, softly at first)*
> To dream the impossible dream,
> To fight the unbeatable foe,
>> *(The other* PRISONERS *join in one by one, their eyes
>> following* CERVANTES)
> To bear with unbearable sorrow,
> To run where the brave dare not go . . .
>
> To run where the brave dare not go,
> Though the goal be forever too far,
> To try, though you're wayworn and weary,
> To reach the unreachable star . . .
>> *(And now the song, swelling in full chorus, over-
>> whelms the "Inquisition Theme")*
> To reach the unreachable star,
> Though you know it's impossibly high,
> To live with your heart striving upward
> To a far, unattainable sky!

*The lights fade out and
the play ends*

A